AFTER THE FLOUNCE

BY
ADENIKE ISENIBI

Published by Icons Media Publishing in 2024

Copyright © Adenike Isenibi

First Edition

The author asserts the moral right under the Copyright, Designs and Patents Act 1988 to be identified as the author of this work.

All Rights reserved. No part of this publication may be reproduced, stored in a retrieval system or transmitted, in any form or by any means without the prior consent of the author, nor be otherwise circulated in any form of binding or cover other than that in which it is published and without a similar condition being imposed on the subsequent purchaser.

PROLOGUE

When I was a little girl my understanding of marriage was as simple and clear as Sunday School proverbs, it hid behind the neat morality slogans: "Love your neighbor as yourself", "love isn't selfish" but it curious to me that couples justify divorce as giving their children peace from their martial conflict while second marriage couples simply justify divorce as a protection of their children (my spouse, their step parents and I don't just agree on parenting, so I have to get them out of there) both rationales in my opinion are really about at least one adult who is afraid to take any further risk to rescue the marriage. More often than not divorce is an act of selfishness not a benevolent action for the wellbeing of the children.

CONTENTS

Chapter One 1

Chapter Two 11

Chapter Three 17

Chapter Four 31

Chapter Five 43

Chapter Six..51

Chapter Seven 61

Chapter Eight 77

Chapter Nine 93

Chapter Ten 101

Chapter Eleven..107

Chapter Twelve 113

Chapter Thirteen 125

Chapter Fourteen...133

Chapter Fifteen..139

Chapter Sixteen...147

Chapter Seventeen 169

CHAPTER ONE

KIKI POV

The three of us sat in a small space in mammi market having our lunch.

I, a graduate of journalism, Samantha Onabanjo, a graduate of Mass communication and Temisan Gregory, the most handsome Medical doctor I have ever seen.

I gazed at him for a moment, thinking how fit, healthy and graciously endowed he looks, as he sat across the table, carefully devouring his meal (Indomie noodles, Egg and Chapman).

Temisan is from Delta State Nigeria but lived most part of his life in the United States of America and of course had all his education over there.

He is so masculine that most women found him appealing,

even overwhelming and irresistible as I have noticed; He was considered to be one of the most handsome men in the NYSC camp.

Samantha Onabanjo is a couple of year older than I, she joined her parents in Abuja immediately we graduated from school.

We have been friends right from our university days.

She had been engaged with a diamond ring by her secondary school sweetheart Oluwatimileyin Durojaiye, a business guru from a very wealthy family.

"It's such a beautiful ring Kiki, I can't wait to show it to you babe" She had told me over the phone with so much excitement.

"I am very happy for you my girl" I replied her screaming and jumping in excitement. Yeah! Really happy for her, when it comes to my friends hooking up with guys I don't have any problem with it, but when it comes to me it's becomes a huge disaster…. Huh? Don't ask me why I really don't know.

Sam was always assuring me before our NYSC camp that she would do anything possible to have me observe my service year in the same city with her.

When we were in school she shared everything she had with me.

It was nice for me to have such a loyal best friend

There's something very special about her "Orekelewa" (piece of beauty) I called her, because she is a piece of beauty both inside and outside, filled with sunshine, light-hearted, kind and compassionate, her love for God and His things is beyond measure.

Sam is tall, elegant and pretty, she simply has the structure of a model

I remember our GST lecturer looked at her one day during one of his full house lectures and said in his deep voice "what will you be doing after graduation?, I sincerely think you should be a model, you'll make a lot of money"

We all laughed and gave her the name Agbani Darego

She has a serious side though, much wiser than all the friends I have ever made, she has this serious way of telling you what she thinks about everything including your own life.

"You have to stop chasing all the men that come to ask you out Kiki, don't you want to get married someday abi na Reverend sister you won be?" (Do you want to become a Reverend Sister)

She would scream at me, pray for me, and at times plead with me.

"All hail the Armageddon, I have heard you, I'd look into it, I will try to make her laugh to get her off my back".

Sam and Temisan are first cousins but had met for the first time at the airport when Sam and her parents went to pick him up a week before the NYSC camp.

My name is Okikiola Olaobaju, I was born and bred in the city of Lagos Nigeria, my family and friends call me Kiki, only my lovely grandma (Iya Agba) calls me by my full name Okikiolamihan.

I am now in Abuja for my NYSC and hoping to be based here after my service year, where I will like to work in a media house as a News caster.

With the exception of my grandmother no one in my family ever thought I would amount to anything, my mum dumped me with my paternal grandmother when I was barely fifteen.

My dad disappeared into thin air after the death of my brother

Aunty Jolaade, my uncle's wife picked me up from the village to stay with her family in Lagos after almost spending one year with iya Agba.

Iya agba visited once in a while, that is the only time Aunty Jola would be nice to me.

"*oshe run re ni Okikiola* " your hair is looking so rough,

iya agba asked me during one of her visits to my uncle's house in Lagos, I would look from mama to Aunty Jola and she would eye me with disgust written all over her unattractive wrinkled face.

"*emadaloun* mama, *omonati lazy ju*" aunty Jola said

"I didn't have the time to make it over the weekend mama, you know my jamb exam is at the corner, and I need to study very hard to make you proud".

"But it won't take you up to two hours to get a simple style done

Ok Iya Igando, I will get it fixed tomorrow"

"*ko si wahala kolou ji wa re maba e dimole shotigbo*"

"*Beeni, iya agba motigbo*, thank you ma"

I dare not tell mama that I don't even attend the Jamb extra moral classes she paid for neither can I tell her that I have not even being given a proper meal not to talk of making my hair.

Despite all the suffering I was still attractive and very intelligent that most people refer to me as a genius.

I could swear that I will have my paradise forever.

Our home was such a paradise on earth, we were not too rich but poverty was far from us.

We were so happy together, just the four of us Dad, mum, Olami and I.

I was pampered beyond description; I was made to believe that I am a Queen.

Until the day the Devil came in, stole my paradise, killed my brother, sent my father away and left my mother miserable.

My teenage years was filled with loneliness, pain and abuse

Aunty Jola abused me, made me do what was far beyond my power

I worked like an Egyptian slave in aunty Jola's house. Uncle Ambrose was never around.

My parents didn't pay any attention to me, I didn't even get to hear from my dad, and my mum would burst in once in a while. Talking to her about my ordeal was never a good idea because she didn't always have anything to say about it.

My growth or what I will be in life never seemed to cross their minds.

My elder brother Olamiposi died at 18, I was told the sad news when I got back from the boarding house a day after my graduation from the secondary school.

"How did this happen mum?"

"Honey, he had an accident and we rushed him to the hospital immediately, but the doctors couldn't save my son they couldn't" she said and broke down in tears.

"Just like that Lami? What happened to you?" I ran into his room and grabbed his picture

I spoke angrily at the picture as if Olami was there with me.

"Why did you have to leave us Lami? You told me you were going to be the greatest Psychologist in the world, you were already working towards it brother, just two years into your dream and you gave up the fight like that? Who did this to you? Who cut short your glory? Who poured water into your burning fire? Who, Lami who?"

I laid on my bed, broken and deeply grieved, I could neither eat nor drink for days.

Then my mum dropped another bomb shell we were leaving without my dad

"Honey we have to leave" my mum said looking tired and lost, her eye balls as red as blood

"I don't get it mom?" Where are we going to? It's been three days since I entered this house from school and dad isn't home yet, did he travel?

"I don't know dear"

"what do you mean you don't know mum?"

"You see" she continued without looking at me "you are no more a baby and you just have to take all of these as they come alright, your dad isn't coming back" she said in a more depressing tone

"Why mom? Is he dead too?"

She turned and looked at me with a wicked smile that brought out her thought "is he not better off dead"

"Look dearie, we don't have money to maintain this", She gave a cursory look around the living room.

That was the last sane conversation I had with my mom.

After then she became mute , not mute as in not able to talk but she had only one answer to all the consolation anybody had to give her, *motigbo* (I have heard)

Always keeping a straight face, no one could reach her or know what was on her mind; she built a strong wall of sadness around herself that no one could pull down. I knew she was going through a lot, I knew she was in pain, "but how can anyone help you mom if you are not ready to be helped" I said to myself.

She remained inconsolable, iya agba tried all she could to console her, she would just smile and tell her "*maami motigbo*, I will be alright", but she was never alright. The unexpressed pain kept eating deep in to her.

I woke up one morning in the village and didn't meet her she was gone.

"iya agba where is my mum", I asked feeling abandoned and deserted.

"She has gone to her friend's residence in Calabar".

I was no stranger anymore to this unspeakable loss and grief; somehow I managed to hide my heartaches and tears of pain.

Adenike Isenibi

CHAPTER TWO

KIKI POV

I ran as fast as my legs could carry me along the street, panting like a wounded dog to aunty Jola's shop. On my knees I said with joy "aunty see my admission letter", she looked at me with disgust and let out a wicked laugh "*aaaah emaawomo yi ke* you are bringing your admission letter to me, to do what with it? I don't have a dime to send you to any school o. You better go to the village and ask Iya agba where your mother is, maybe she will be able to foot your fees if not", she bent her neck, eyed me and hit the back of her right hand to the inside of her left to complete her statement.

"After all the slavery I did in your house aunt, the sleepless night, when your baby will be tied to my back and sitting down became a bad idea, I will have to dance,

dance and dance to make her sleep, sometimes it took me more than three hours into the middle of the night, when everyone must have been fast asleep and then I will have to wake up before everyone else to start cooking for your kids getting them ready for school the next morning". I thought painful tears running down my face as I walked sadly back home.

I entered the small church on our street and prayed before setting out for the village. " Dear God at this point it is only you and my grandma that I have, I know you can hear me now, please don't let me drop out of school, I don't know how my tuition fees is going to be paid but I know you will send someone to me to pay this money, my mum always included in the various names she called you that you are a present help in times of trouble, I believe you are and I know you will not fail me now"

I went to the village to meet mama with a heavy heart; it took me several minutes to enter the gate.

Finally I summoned the courage to enter, I was expecting her to say "Okikiola my daughter maybe we should go and register you to learn a trade as your Aunty Jolaade had advised"

My eyes widened and slowly my lips curved with a smile as I heard "don't worry Okikiola , I have broken my Esusu you will get your fees paid before the school's resumption you don't have to be sad, you have always made me proud just like your father, very intelligent", she said with tears in her eyes.

She turned and held me "I will see you attain your dreams in life"

"mo le ma jeun abi kin rasho sugbon olo le iwe re omo mi"

I hugged mama tightly with tears of joy flowing down my face, looked to heaven with a smile and whispered "God I know this you, thank you"

Mama struggled to pay all my fees, I went to school most times without any money aside my fees but here I am today. Even though it was tough and rough, at 22 I am a graduate.

I can look back and say I owe it to God and my grandmother, my angel here on earth.

***

I was startled back to life by Sam's hand on my shoulder.

"Kiki, Kiki Kiki haaa sup are you here with us"

"Yea sure guys, just day dreaming I guess", I said smiling to her

"Day dreaming? She replied humorously I don't think so madam, this expression on your face plus talking to yourself looks more of noon mare to me", she laughed and got up, "let me get my phone and join you guys shortly" she tapped Temi at the back

"Aii girl" he answered with his American accent.

She hadn't even left for a second when Temisan who had been pretending I don't exist, raised his head and grabbed my hands.

"Kiki let's start dating" he said, my eyes shot out in surprise

This guy must really be full of himself, oboi what a spoilt brat, "is this what you say to women where you are coming from? I thought you boasted of being a born again Christian, I asked in anger "you just see a girl and walk up to her and say let's start dating?

"Yeahhhh" he shrugged, "I mean I know you like me and I'm sure I like you too".

"'WHAT!" I exclaimed standing on my feet "that is the most arrogant statement I have heard in this 21stcentury, I advise you go get some manners., Jesus! you are damn too proud". I eyed him and walked away, he ran after me and apologized

"Kiki please wait! , ok am an asshole"

"I'm sorry ok please"

"Why don't you wanna give us a chance?'

"There's no us Temisan, will you please let me be!"

'Well, this is probably a wrong timing" he said almost whispering to himself.

"How about me coming to your hostel later so we can talk"?

"How about you never coming to border me again proud man" I fired back and fled towards the NYSC female dorm before he could open his mouth to annoy me further.

Adenike Isenibi

CHAPTER THREE

TEMI POV

Dear diary: *worst day ever! I lost my hero and my brother*

I trusted you, you were my best friend, how could you even think of leaving without telling me, how could you do this to your princess and the woman that you said you loved so much, at the worse time of their lives, I didn't know you to be this mean, you taught me to be kind and always considerate, how can I face the fact that you are not here again and that you might not be coming back, you taught me to be strong, but I tell you , I'm as weak as a flower detached from it branch, I don't know how to be strong without you, I will never forgive you dad.

Dear diary: *She left me too*

I won't shed any more tears I promise, even though I am missing them so much, I think it is just high time I kept it all behind me because none of them seems to be thinking of how I feel or how I would feel in their absence, it's all good I am going to be ok all by myself. Turning the page, moving on. Goodbye mum.

Dear diary: *Spirituality does not change a man from being a man*

My conclusion is that man is a man even if he is a Bishop.

How can you hit her so hard, I thought you said women are weaker vessels and need to be treated with care and affection and to say that you call yourself a man of God (a pastor). Huh? I will never give any man the privilege to treat me any kind of way NEVER. Mehn I hate you with a passion uncle.

Dear diary: *It is called ere osupa*

I won't say I love it here but this part; I am enjoying so much, stories about animals, about olden days and our fore fathers

Gram has such a wild imagination. You are a good story teller; thumb up to you my very lovely iya agba.

Dear diary: *I do not like it here at all*

I didn't know it was a journey to slavery when iya agba said I will be going back with uncle Ambrose to stay with his family, Auntie Jola, seemed all nice when she was in the village, I thought I was free from village foods, weird kind of behaviours from different corners, "I will sure miss you ere osupa" my statement three weeks ago the previous night I was leaving the village. Well it has been work, work and over work since I got here, sleeping very late at night is definitely not my style but I don't seems to have any choice now, do I?

Aunte Jola is just a task master.

Dear Diary*: this one is a letter to my mum and dad*

How I long to feel your touch mom, I long to hear your sweet melodious voice singing and teaching me how to sing, I am longing to eat those delicious delicacies of yours.

Mummy do you remember those days when you would persuade me to have my meals.

Remember the day I resumed at the boarding house you met my guardian and pleaded with her to watch my eating habit

"Mom will you please stop embarrassing me" I said covering my face with both hands

And Dad supported me with a loud laugh "yeah you heard her, stop embarrassing my princess ok"

You hugged me like a million times and begged me "baby please eat your meals"

Just for you to let me be I told you, "ok mom I will"

Annoyingly you pushed further. "Are you promising me?"

"Yeah mom I cross my heart", I said rolling my big eye balls like my father's

You can't believe how hungry I am now. The black and always shinny hair of mine is breaking shorter each day, it has even changed colour to brown, your little Angel's beautiful dresses have all turned to rags

Where are you my African queen, my first best friend, my song angel? I still can't believe you are not here with me.

How I wish you can change your mind and come back to me, remember the happy family we once had.

Daddy my Angel Michael please come out from your hiding place and go look for your love, bring her back so we can be a happy family again.

Mum remember those days we will act "Alien and the Angel" together just the four of us, you, daddy, Olamiposi and I.

You played the role of the song angel, I was the little beautiful princess, daddy was our angel Michael and

Olami was dad's ADC. They defended us when aliens came to steal the beautiful princess.

Remember those songs you use to sing for Angel Michael and his ADC to descend from the sky to save us from aliens and I stayed at one corner in the sitting room giggling with happiness, when our angels start descending from the staircase, dressed in white regalia and moving their hands like birds.

Coming towards the sitting room's door they would remove their daggers made of wood pretending to be killing the aliens.

Oh God why will you allow the wicked Devil to steal my paradise.

> *Oh what a world I've come to stay!*
> *Oh what a taste of sweet to soar!*
> *Oh what can I do to feel better?*
> *Oh I feel so terrible within*

> *Life has taken from a Paradise*
> *Life has shown me pains*
> *Life has shredded my heart to pieces*
> *Life has broken my bones*

I reach out to you my saviour

Save oh please Saviour save

Save me from this cold world

Where loneliness is the song, I sing.

Do parents even know what their divorce really cost their children?

Your divorce takes from us our paradise, our pride.

It takes our sense of belonging

It has taken from us the right to a good life

It takes from us a right to good education

Some of us are stack illiterates; we are very angry with ourselves, you our parents and even with our creator

We cannot express ourselves, we are not allowed to.

No one wants to listen to what we have to say.

No one is kind enough to check how we are truly feeling

Some of us are dying, others are long gone, we are hungry, some of us are naked, we have been brutally abused, we have been insulted, we have been alleged falsely, we have turned thieves in our own father's house, many of us have taken the root of prostitution, many are with dangerous weapons forcefully collecting what do not belong to them

We have been pushed; many of us have lost their lives, looking for love in wrong places.

Many of us are living a life of stigma, many of us are still crying for help.

Many of us have so many questions and nobody to answer them.

> *When your heart has so many questions*
> *When you don't know the one to ask*
> *How do you even put them in words?*
> *When your enemies are celebrating*
> *When victory seems lost.*
> *How do you even carry on?*

> *When I can't find the one that holds the peace*
> *When I just feel like giving up the fight*
> *When I can't hold the trophy up high*
> *How do I even complete this race?*

It really not easy for us mummy and daddy, we are not finding all of these funny at all. We have to eat little even if we still yearn for more, we have to do what is far too much more than our little bones, some of us are committing suicide, some have even ran to strange lands.

Daddy and Mummy don't you think, it is the right time

to save these innocent souls. Save us we are suffering so much please save us.

We need you to retrospect on the things that attracted you to each other and comeback together again.

Do you know that as long as you are apart, our lives are prone to destruction?

Take a look at what daily success email #227 wrote

A child's initial perception of God is based largely on his/her experience with their parents

When parents are divorced, they are displaying attitudes and actions that are contrary to God, which can have a serious and devastating repercussion in their lives.

Many children picture God as someone who is distant and uninterested in their daily lives, a God who will leave them during hard times or an angry God, who watches for things to punish

In a divorce, children are often forced to choose sides with one parent or the other, this can be a spiritual tragedy, because children are to honour their father and mother so that things will go well with them.

Honour thy father and thy mother as the Lord thy God hath commanded thee

That thy day maybe prolonged and that it may go well with thee

In the land the Lord thy God giveth thee

Deuteronomy 5:16 (kjv)

Also when children are forced to live with one parent and visit another, they are placed under dual authorities, this result to confusion for these children.

I read to detail the diary that Kiki left on the chair, "wow this is deep" I said and left the shade to look for Samantha.

"Sam, thank goodness I found you at last, where on earth have you been, I have been looking all over the camp for you"

"Come, come, come" I pulled her along with me out of the crowd to a corner of the football field

"I think I know the reason your friend Kiki doesn't want anything to do with any guy".

"How? What do you mean, wise one", She teased

"Here take a look at this"

"Diary, what's this about?"

"Sam I was talking to Kiki as planned, she got angry and left, I went after her coming back to wait for you and saw this on the chair she was sitting on".

"Why don't you just read first?"

"Did you read her diary Temi?" Samantha asked me motherly

"Yeah Sam I had to, I mean can't you see the abnormality in Kiki's behaviour , it's just been two weeks I met her but I tell you that, that behaviour of hers isn't normal, I think she is angry about something sis, she gets lost when you are trying to make a conversation with her; she attacks even little stuff with anger"

"But it's not still right bro, I think it's better we make her talk to us instead of intruding her privacy like this" Sam said waving the black diary.

Well "the talk" you have not been able to get her to talk since all these years Sam" I said and made a sad face

"Just read please"

"Alright! Alright! " Sam said and raised her hands in surrendering "oh I see, now I know what the problem is with you, Kiki. I knew there was more to "my parents got separated, I was taken to my grams at fifteen and my brother died at eighteen" she nodded slowly as she finished reading.

"We have to help her in any way we can Sam, I think she is suffering and I love this girl with all my heart babe" I said to an angry Sam

"Yeah Temi, we will sure get her out of this" she waved the black dairy and turned furiously towards the female dorm

"Sam wait up!" I called after her

"Please don't go to her like that, come on, I mean none of these is her fault, why are you racing to meet her in that mood, wait lets pray for her before you go"

You will not understand bro, I know her more than she knows herself the only way you can make her understand a thing is to wear a serious look, I have prayed for her, fasted because of her, begged her, joked and even have gone as far as match making her with guys, but it has always been this same old story, " I don't like that guy Sam; he is arrogant, he is too short, too fair, too tall or he does not know how to treat his woman right" she mimicked Kiki, "now I have to take it the serious way" Sam said as she continued walking towards the girls dormitory.

"Sam, Sam" I called again trying to convince her further.

"I'd see you later Temi" She said without looking back.

***

KIKI POV

As I sat under the tree watching the to and fro movement of the Corp Members I realized I have something for Temi, "OMG!!! Is it that obvious? Kiki you cannot possibly be in love with Temisan" I scolded myself, what!!! That rude guy! naaaaa, I am not allowing myself to fall for any man much less a proud one like him. Guys are the same, arrogant, selfish, sneaky, cunny snakes.

The phone in my waist purse rang, interrupting my train of thought, startled out of my day dreaming which has now become my best companion, reaching for it, I picked and heard Sam voice at the other end

"Sup Sam"

"I'm cool, where are you?"

"Under the big tree near the girls' dorm"

"Alright will be there in a sec"

"Alright cool".

I shifted to make space for Samantha, who isn't looking anywhere near being happy. What could possibly be wrong with her now? We were silent for some couple of minutes.

"'Sup girl, have you gotten your phone?" I said, trying to break the uncomfortable silence between us.

No, I used wood to call you. She said with a frown

"Aaaah what have I done again naw, are you okay babe?"

"I am good" she answered sharply

"Okay then if you insist. But babe , that your cousin is such a pain in the neck"

"What did he do to you?" Samantha eyed me dubiously

"He is a proud guy, Jeez!!!"

"Guess what he told me when you left us to collect your phone "yeah Kiki let's start dating, because I know you like me" can you imagine?"

Samantha shook her head and got up furiously. It was as if I poured fuel into a burning fire

"You know something Kiki I think you are going to end up an angry old maid, maybe you will just wake up one morning and see that you are fifty years old and you've chased all the men around you".

"You will end up staying alone in a house far from the town and people will start calling you an old witch, what is your problem Kiki, huh what is it?, are you the only one that will not have her parents together, is that why you want to destroy your life and other people's happiness?, if your parents have decided they don't want to stay together again, must you now mortgage your own life for those that don't even know if you are alive, dead or gone on an exile, people that don't know how you have made it up to this stage of your life, you think I don't know? I got this from Temisan, your "black calendar, black book or whatever you call it, you left it on the seat when you were doing what you know how to do best scaring all the men away selfish girl"

She threw it on my lap and walked away

I fell silent; my lips parted as if words had frozen on my tongue, tears came running down my face.

"OMG how could I have been so careless". I said finally with clinched teeth.

CHAPTER FOUR

KIKI POV

I felt the need to apologise, I knew the feeling was ridiculous because none of this was my fault but it was ingrained in me the need to apologise for everything, I couldn't help it, I wanted to be happy and everybody too, most especially I didn't want to ever lose my best friend Samantha, not been in talking terms with her for two days felt like forever.

After much rehearsal I summoned courage to call her

"Hello Sam!"

"Hey" she replied in a cold tone

"Where are you?"

"Mamii market, same corner"

"Alright I will be there shortly'

Oh God I don't have the courage to face Temi yet pleeee-aaaasssseeee, I made a small prayer to God, "he will not be there oh sweet Jesus"

God answered my prayer as I sat quickly to talk to Sam before Temi would probably show up.

"Babes I am here to apologise, I......."

She interrupted me, "I'm so sorry too Kiki I think I overreacted, I mean who am I to judge you like that, I just didn't know how to make you understand that you deserve to be happy", Sam said looking away to fight back her tears.

"It's ok babe" I stretched my hands to hug her, "I am going apologise to Temi and will also date him too if that will make you happy", Sam's lips curved in a small faint smile.

"No Kiki don't date Temisan because you want to make me happy, I think you should follow your heart. If you don't want him babes it's cool, but be sure I won't push you into something bad alright, listen with the little time I have spent with Temi, what he has gisted me about himself and his way of life, he might not be the most disciplined of all men but he is a very good guy and I know he is in love with you Kiki"

"Thanks babe", I gave her another hug "I will follow my heart ma'am, the dean of love faculty" I said in a deep tone and gave her a bow.

She laughed out loud and pushed me away

"You don't want to know how much I have missed you for this past two days and I'm promising it will never happen again", Sam said placing a hand of on my left shoulder.

"BF Forever mehn" I said and we hugged again, this time for a long time

"There's something else I have been meaning to ask you babe" Sam said with a serious look.

"What is it, am I in trouble again?" I said smiling

"No jare" she hissed and gave me a mild punch on the chest

"Like seriously babe, what really happened between your Mum and Dad?"

I took a deep breath, let out a sign and started talking

"Babe I don't know what exactly, none of them said anything, but I have this strong feeling it has something to do with the death of my brother"

"How babe? Didn't you ask any of them?" Sam asked in a sad tone

"Believe me I did, I had this huge quarrel with my mum five years ago but despite my anger and threat not to ever talk to her again if she refused to tell me what broke our home, she didn't tell me anything"

"Mehn this is an odd situation" Sam said folding her two hands at the back of her head. "But hey I think you should forget them and live your life; if they want you they will somehow find their way back into your life ok"?

"Yeah babe" I said gratefully.

"Don't expose yourself to more pain, do you understand?"

"Yeah" I nodded obediently

"They have done enough to you, they broke your heart, ruined your childhood, don't allow their carelessness rob you of the happy life you are about to have, Kiki you deserve to be happy, you have a heart of gold, you are pretty and kind-hearted and most of all you know God and fear him, I want you to always have it mind that God got your back at all times, , He will not allow anything bad to happen to you, Look Temisan is just the man you need right now, someone who will give you the kind of life you deserve"

She held of my hands and squeezed them

"Yeah I think you are right Sam" I said

"I will give it a trial"

"I'll give Temi a chance"

"Seriously?" she asked excitedly

"Yeah seriously"

Hmmn that is so cool babes, she gave me a happy hug again, picked up her phone and jumped out of the shade.

I turned some minutes later to see what she was up to and saw her dancing on the phone.

"I know you are calling your brother, Temi"

She made a face at me, smiled and walked away.

***

What an awesome feeling, that feeling - that comes when nothing else matters , a feeling of finally reaching the place where you belong, that feeling when you can only imagine concentration when he is either around you or you are thinking about him.

Temi and I became involved romantically.

I have never felt this way before; he showered on me all the love a woman will ever require from a man, we were always together.

We left the camp after three weeks and were posted to different places in the heart of the city of Abuja; he would always bring my launch to my office and come back in the evening to pick me up to the house. He would often take me out on weekends to the garden and while he plays his guitar I would sing love songs. How can I show God how grateful I am, because this can only be his handiwork.

Temisan pampered me, he cleared the bad memory and the anger I have been carrying for years. Wow I didn't know love could feel this good, so there is still a man that can be this nice. He played a lot of love songs for me with his box guitar on several occasions. Every moment with him was an experience I treasure a lot.

On a particular Sunday, Temi invited me over to his family house to have dinner with them. On getting to this beautiful mansion, the entire family members were in front of the entrance to welcome me. Approaching the entrance, a soothing fragrance received me. I was astonished by the well arranged interiors. We all went straight to the dining table well decorated with varieties of food on it. We began to eat after the father blessed the food. I started noticing that all eyes were on me, little whispers here and there, then I became uncomfortable, I became shy. Then the mother broke the silence and said "she's so beautiful" then immediately, his sisters nodded their heads to show their affirmation. I was just able to say "thank you" when words finally came out of my mouth.

"Which part of the country do you come from" asked the father.

"Kwara state sir" I replied.

"What do your parents do for a living?" the mother asked.

Then, I began stuttering because I didn't even know where my parents were. Then I remembered, "My father is an accountant" I said.

"You are highly welcome my dear, would you mind telling us about you background|" asked the father.

At this point, I lost my appetite, and became speechless, Temi then rescued me and broke the silence,

"Dad that's not something she likes to remember, especially not now, but the summary is that her parents are separated while she was still young, so she grew up with her grandmother".

Then I sigh of relieve within me, thanks to Temi for saving me. Suddenly, I noticed a strange look on the mother's face. She didn't even finish her food before leaving the dining to her room.

After the dinner, we went to the living room. I began to notice that something was going wrong. The father left too, and then the sisters also left to their room. Only Temi and I were remaining in the living room, later Temi was called by his mum, then I began to hear their loud whispers.

"Look, you can't bring this girl to this house|" said the mum.

"Why not mum|"

"How can you bring in a girl without base? She has no background; she's from a broken home. Let me tell you little about such girls that grew up without a father or mother. Children who did not grow with their parents as a result of divorce, separation, death, tight schedule and abandonment will have problem of insecurity, sound decision making, they will find it difficult to form lasting relationship and consequently they will have marital challenges. Her own case is even worse, no father, no mother. 85% of behaviour disorders come from fatherless children, 85% of youths in prison are from a fatherless home, 75% 0f patients in chemical abuse centres come from fatherless homes, I can go on and on. I can't allow my grand children to be brought up by such a girl. No, not while I'm alive."

"But mum, what about her own personalities. This girl is not a wayward girl, even in the midst of all these tendencies you've listed; she has managed to keep herself in the right path. Why should children like her suffer for what their parents did? I love her so much and mum if you insist, I won't get married again.

"Hey hey, you both stop this madness. Sweetheart why are you talking like this. Yes I agree that most children from such background could have these problems, but not all. There are some of them that are even having better morals than children brought up by their parents. I am sure you have not forgotten that my mother was in her shoes, but despite all she went through, I tell you I was brought up pretty well, I can boldly stand anywhere in the world and shout it loud that my mother is the best mom in the universe, If you insist on this, then you are indirectly saying that my mum is also wayward. What I saw in that young girl is an excellent daughter in-law; her character is no way close to those characters you've mentioned." The father intervened.

"Thank you daddy, please make her understand that it's either is this girl or it's no one else" Temi said and rushed out, grabbed my right hand "baby, let's go".

I picked up my bag with my wet face I ran in to the car and was crying profusely.

"Look baby, I'm sorry about all that ok. See, nothing will change my mind. I love you and that's all I know"

I could not utter a word, could not stop crying. He drove me back to my house and wanted to stay with me for a while, but I insisted he leaves.

I laid on the bed and started rolling from one side to the other, what a blast from the past. So after all my parents made me passed through, I'm also going to share the consequences of their actions? What a world I found myself. While I began a fresh cry, I remembered the story of Queen Esther and Ruth in the Holy Bible. I remembered that the place that God is taking me is a place of honour, a place of grace and a place of favour. There, my background doesn't matter, my upbringing does not matter, and my past cannot stop me. Then my heart was consoled, I prayed, handed everything to God and slept off.

Few days later his mom visited

She told me that Temi had been betrothed to one of their political friends' daughter since they were teenagers.

"If he's ever going to rule his father's country he will have to make acquaintances politically and trust me the only stress less way is for him to marry this girl, the thing now is that, he has accepted to marry this girl after so much talk but his worried that his decision will hurt you, that's why I have come to beg for you to let Temi go, let him fulfill his dream, he has been chosen let him reign please" she said and fell on her knees in my room.

I quickly rushed to help her up " its alright ma'am ,I will let him be, intact I'm going away far from here " I assured her with a heavy heart.

"Thank you so much" she smiled revealing the

wickedness behind her pretty face as she wrapped her arms around my stiff body.

"Look you can have this" she brought out a swollen paper bag.

"This is a million naira"

"What are you paying me for ma'am?

" No,no, I'm not paying you for anything, I just want you to use this as your transport fare" she pacified me.

"That won't be necessary ma'am, I can take care of myself" I said as a painful smile escaped my lips.

I packed my things and left, I left my heartbeat, I left my reason to live behind.

Adenike Isenibi

CHAPTER FIVE

KIKI POV

I can't believe it's four years already that I left the sore of this country, back briefly to Nigeria three days ago for the business establishment and our political party's inauguration.

And the thought of logging into my social media accounts came to mind, first I installed Facebook and clicked on forgot password as it helped me search for my account through my email.

I sat in front of my computer punching the keys as if slaughtering a mortal enemy, getting rid of bastard's pictures on my Facebook page, I didn't know those pictures were still there, the severed pain these guys left in heart, the past came rushing in my brain.

I remember every hash word and bad behavior of that heartless human called Dan, the one I thought would help hold my raised arm of second chance on love, but he turned out to be worse than the one I gave my love to at first, the one I called my first love, he shattered my heart into pieces and went further to cut the pieces into some smaller pieces.

But why was I even surprised when he tongue-lashed me again the day I went to see him after the three months of us not talking, as soon as I heard his car engine I pretended to be sleeping.

Daniel Smith the proud one had walked in with his stiff neck, studied me and smirked, his thought written boldly on his face "I knew you will come back, you always do"

He went to the dinning table to some well prepared delicious delicacies gracing it as my eyes traveled after him.

He walked back to me to me and tapped me on my right leg, I grumbled and opened one of my eyes, saw him standing and close it back again, waiting for his apology to make me fully awake but instead it was his rude statement that made me jump out of my pretentious wonderland.

"What are you doing here, I thought someone said they don't want to see me again"

"I don't understand"

"What part don't you understand" his two hands in he pockets looking around proudly.

"You mean you want to waste this opportunity to apologize for your unruly act?" I asked almost screaming.

"What untruly act is she even talking about?"

"You hit me Dan" I refreshed his memory.

"Well I did and ?" He shrugged to complete his statement.

I smiled and looked away fighting back the tears that gathered in my eyes " wow such arrogance "

Dan moved a little bit too close to comfort and said "you know you can't come to my house and call me names right, its totally unacceptable"

I stepped back, talking to myself " but Kiki what are you doing here?

Dan frowned, smiled,walked away and over his head "now that you have your senses back, please close my door behind you"

"Rude bastard" I said between clinched teeth as I pace beside my bed in my hotel room

I remembered again how it started and ended between me and Dan the girlfriend beater, all I went through before leaving the shore of this country.

Fresh tears climbed down my face in my small room that year in Auntie B's house when Dan added salt to the injury Temi left in my heart, a persistent knock interrupted my train of thought, I dragged my feet to the door, opened to reveal

"From frying pan to fire, oh God what is Toni doing here" my thought was loud

Toni my rude and blunt cousin, escaped ugly by just an inch, walked pass me nonchalantly pass me to the bed.

"You're alive, I called a million times"

She stopped dead in her track as though just remembered something then looked at me "what happened, who died?" She added a sarcastic smile

I walked up to her and sat on a chair next to the bed where she was sitting.

"Listen Tee the last thing I need right now is your tricky sarcasm alright"

"And who is been sarcastic, you said you were done for good this time, how come I'm seeing this puffy eye balls hun"

"I..I..er" I stammered not sure if Toni was the best candidate for my truth airing.

"You err er what" Toni mimicked mockingly.

"I went to see him" I said quickly hiding my face from her

Toni looked at me in shock "you can't seriously be talking about cavalier Dan" she bent her neck to my face seeking answer

"Yes I said hastily before I changed my mind about letting out the truth.

Toni's popped out eye balls roamed my face for a while.

" Yes Kiki?, you're an idiot true, no wonder the self asserting, presuming, overweening idiot, decorated lunatic beats you up like a goat at will and doesn't even see anything wrong in it, you went to see him , for what if I may ask"

I looked at her searching explanation for my stupidity

"I don't know, I don't know I treated him badly I guess, I didn't give him a chance to explain himself, I felt guilty and I.."

"Shut up please, just shut up, what explanation does a woman beater has? And do you think it's guilt you feel each time you run into the arms of that monster, its not guilt, its foolishness."

"Well forgive me if I don't want to loose my second relationship, forgive me if I'm tired of rejection, forgive if...."

"Which relationship" she interrupted me with a wave of hand "is that what you call a relationship or a situationship, you're enslaving yourself each time you run back to that guy, wake up Kiki that guy will kill you one day"

I swiped my face with the back of my palm, Lord give me strength to deal with this, I can't do Toni right now, as much as her rebuke is filled with obvious truth, there's enough on my plate already, please help me' I said a quick prayer in my thought

I walked to the bed to Toni, held her up and pushed her mildly towards the door.

"Okay thanks for coming, remember you work on Saturday"

"Not any more, see! Dan won't even allow you check on fam"

"Okay my bad, still I wan to be left alone, come and be going biko (please)"

"You're asking me out of your house"

"No buddy, I'm asking you to give me space to figure things out" I pushed her further out of the door and closed it, then the closed door opened as I was about to turn around Toni poked her head in the half opened door "okay I'm going enjoy your pity party"

"Thank you, just go away and let me wallow in my self pity" I replied slammed the door behind her and walked to the kitchen to prepare the food I knew I won't be able to eat.

The humming of my favorite song died prematurely as I walked out of the shower and beheld Auntie Jane starring at me as if about to pounce on me

Auntie B I called her, was my mom best friend, she's been a mother and friend since I left Abuja to Calabar, she had gone to Uyo for a three day shopping for her provision shop.

"Auntie B, you're back"

"Yes I am " she answered me frowning

"Oh okay I thought you were supposed to come back tomorrow"

"So that you can still have one more day to wallow in your self pity right?"

"What do you mean..oh that loud speaker has called you right?"

"Yes she has, is she lying?, answer me if she is, why did you go there again Kiki?"

"But auntie B.."

"Shut up Kiki, what's your problem hun?"

"Auntie I'm tired of rejection""

I folded my arms, hugging my self half backing my auntie B like a spoilt child, we became silent for a while then she said finally

"Okikimi" she said and gathered me into her arms, as I broke down in tears

"Don't shed any more tears my child, listen all these rejection is God setting you up for a great place where those that rejected you can't go with you, you have a good heart, why don't you wait patiently and give that person that deserves it, I can't pretend not to see all that have been going on, I see the pain, I see you trying to force a smile, I see those unshed tears, I see your struggle, I see it all" she held my face to hers " remember that your quote"

""You cannot fail until you quit" we shouted it loud together "

Laughed and tightened our hug

"You will soon see the reason you've had to go through all you went through"

"Thank you auntie"

CHAPTER SIX

KIKI POV

It was those days I had the urge to write but didn't just know how to start, I stared at my laptop screen, hiding inside my closet, one of the annoying things I used to in those days when I didn't know what to do, I finally decided to watch a movie in it.

A knock on the door as Lix let himself in,

Lix is my Auntie B's son and only child, I stood and walked from the closet to him

"Oh Lix its you, good morning bro"

"You and this your closet ehn"

"Lemme jareh"

"I knocked but no answer, I could go and come.back if its a bad time" he said as he gazed at my puffy face.

"No its alright, don't mind me I will be okay"

"Good,,because you have to e okay to enjoy this good news I'm about to share with you"

I sat up eagerly staring at Lix's lips for the words to drop.

"So my boss likes your work and the job of a creative director is yours, if not too sudden for my celebrity writer and doc then she will be resuming on Monday"

"What did you say Lix"

"You heard me"

the smile on my face lit the atmosphere, I stood and jumped on him excitedly

"Oh Lix I'm so excited about this, I can't wait for Monday to come"

"Great then congratulations?"

"Alright thanks so we should go and celebrate, I, you and Auntie B"

"Hmmm you guys will have to go and celebrate without me, I have a date" he said got up and walked towards the door.

"Is Presh back?" I asked him

"Nope"

"Who then does Mr Casanova has a date with, hmm take it easy o, Aids is real" I rolled my eyes at him.

"Don't judge me like that Miss, do you know if its a business date or a movie date with one of my friends"

"Yeah right its a movie date with one of your friends, I know" I shook my head and started laughing very hard

"Omg you this girl ehn, thanks for making me laugh anytime I'm with you" he said amidst laughter and hugged me

"Are you joking?, if you know what this your coming has done to me this morning you will know that I'm the one that's supposed to be thanking you"

"I'm.glad you're happy sis, let me run along so that I won't be late for my date"

"Yes, yes run along don't be late for the movie date with er"

"Dave" he helped me out mischievously

We both laughed as he opened the door and jumped out

I walked to the bed and threw my self on it happily.

***

Lix's raised voice came muffled through the pillow I was

hiding under, I made a few grumbly noises and smothered my face down further into the sheets attempting to block his way out, few minutes seemed passed in silence and I began to relax thinking he has given up and walked away instead I felt a cold air hit me as my blanket was ripped off me.

"I've had enough of your childish attitude young lady, your first day at work and you want yo go late, here goes the first impression"

"How is it morning already, I barely slept for one minute"

"Please stop testing my sanity, get up and get ready, I'm giving you just 10 minutes, if not you will receive the honorable presence of your Auntie B" he walked away as I grumbled to his back.

"How in heaven's name am I going to get ready in 10 minutes?"

"10 minutes young lady, do not let me come back to your room please"

"Oh Lix you're wicked true, whyyyyyy" I screamed into the duvet playfully.

"You will know how wicked I am if you're not ready in 10 minutes" he said and walked further away.

***

Please sit" the chairman said to me nicely

"Thank you sir"

I sat as he handed me an envelope, I opened it immediately and here we are my employment letter, but the most shocking thing is it carries a USA address.

I stretched the letter to him not understanding.

"Yes you're not going to be working with us here in Nigeria, you are our new creative director at our USA branch congratulations once again Miss Johnson

" Jesus " I said excitedly "thanks so much sir"

"Oh thank you Lord, you sure work in amazing ways" I knelt in my thought and raised my hands up high to him.

"So please submit your passport to the HR department before you go today that's if you have it with you of course if you don't then you can bring it tomorrow then"

"Hope its not like I'm dreaming or something" I Left the office and almost injuring my skin from too much pinching.

A knock on the door brought me back to the present day and reminded me of how long I have been there staring at my iPad, I walked to it and welcome the most unwanted trouble of that moment.

"Hello cousin I said if Mohammed doesn't go the

mountain the mountain will come to Mohammed" Toni walked pass me like the owner of my life.

"I thought we agreed on phone yesterday to meet tomorrow evening for a drink which one is now Mohammed and the mountain"

"Did we?" She asked sarcastically again as usual

"Its alright I know you couldn't just wait to see my pretty face again" I said smiling

" Get over yourself madam I remembered that tomorrow is the big day"

"I know but I'm not sleeping there"

"Okay madam get up and let's hit the road"

"Right now?"

"What's your stress though, not like you're paying for anything, we are using my car ad paying for whatever we're having, why are you making it seems like an unfair situation?"

"Haaba naw I'm just tired ni"

"Tired from what"

"From the journey of course"

"The journey you did since three days ago and since then

has been sleeping, my friend get up and go and change or I will drag you along in your pyjamas"

"You dare not"

You know me o" she said and started off towards me

"Okay, okay" I ran towards the wardrobe "And hey you're supposed to be here with the guy you stole from me, where is he?"

"Which guy did I steal from you" she hissed

"My Casanova brother of course"

"His no more a Casanova Kiki, his changed"

"Are you sure cos that guy,hunnn"

"No one can double date on me, I am enough wahala for a guy sis, you're talking as if you don't know me anymore, I'm the only one who hasn't changed, I remain, me"

"Hmm Margaret Tacha herself, I totally forgot who I am standing before, sorry ma" I bowed and she hit me lightly as we both started laughing

Haa Toni a bundle of wahala I quickly changed into a nice short dress and we hit the road, Toni and Lix are the most wonderful host in the universe they took me to a very nice place to relax.

***

TEMI POV

I sat the back of my jeep pressing my iPad early morning news pouring of my car stereo.

"Global approach is the only way to fight Covid 19", UN says as it launches humanitarian response plan"

I shook my head as my phone beeped, I eyed the phone and sighed before picking it .

I lifted it to my ear, heaved a sigh and said tiredly "Hellow mom"

Hello son" Mrs Erica Greg Lewis spoke at the other end as she checked out the wellbeing of her garden flowers

"So how are you" she spoke again

"I'm fine mom, how are you today"

"You didn't come home last night"

"Yeah mom I was at Paul's "

"Okay are you on your way home now?"

"No mom I have something urgent to do at the office"

"What urgent stuff can't wait for the boss, Temi you're driving this your engine too hard o"

"As long as it can still be driven I don't mind mom"

"Hmm just like his father, come back early the lockdown is starting soon"

"We don't know for sure yet mom"

"It's certain son"

"Okay mom, I will know my way back if they announce it, I have a lot of stuff to do, I mean you know I have just three months on this business established before I head back to the state and those partners from the USA aren't complaining about the lockdown plus a meeting with the youth leader and I'm official meeting the most talk about powerful woman holding the DPP, I can't keep all of them waiting now ma can I"

"Okay I didn't know they'll be coming today, just take it easy son, so the reason I called ..."

"I haven't forgotten mom" Temi interrupted

"I just wanted to be sure son you know that...."

"Mom I said I remember everything, you told me just three days ago, I have to go now byee"

He punched the end button of the phone and buried his face in his two palm and exhaled.

Adenike Isenibi

CHAPTER SEVEN

KIKI POV

"What's wrong babe you don't look too bright this morning, anything the matter?"

Lix said to me immediately I entered his car and collapsed in the back seat, sighing loudly.

"Could it be about the presentation" Toni asked genuinely concerned

"Hell no" she has been doing this since like ages, not only is she confident in herself, she also delivers always" Lix added boosting my moral.

"Okay mister know my cousin better than me, Weldon sir, but seriously babe are you okay?"

"I'm good dear, sometimes I feel so overwhelmed, I know it can't definitely be the presentation, I mean not like I'm going for an interview or anything, I have drafted the offer no one can reject so it can't be that"

"Wow okay so what is it, ...oohk I know you forgot to pray" Toni said after a short pause

"Of course not I pray every day before anything, honestly its not that I can't really point out what the problem is, but don't worry guys I will be okay"

"Alright then whatever it is know that we are always here for you huh?" Lix said with a serious face

"I know and thanks for having my back always I love you guys very much"

They alighted with me from the car and we did a group hug

"Now run along before you don't have a chance to release the offer they won't be able to reject" Toni said to me as we disengaged.

I adjusted my cloth, exhaled and walked towards the giant glass building my heartbeat sounding like a church bell.

"Hello my name is Miss Okikiola Jadesola Johnson, I have an appointment with TEM holdings" I said to the Receptionist.

She smiled and looked up the computer for my name.

"Yes Miss Jade, to the first floor, the third door by the the right, that's the board room, the management are already there waiting"

I grinned as if the young lady had just added to my nervous breakdown.

I walked away, got to the door opened to reveal a beautiful board room "Omg" I said in my thought as my eye balls popped out ogling the beauty of the well-lit board room and also the well dressed elites I will be working with for the next three months

"Miss Jade Johnson may we have your attention please"

In sweet voice brought me back to life.

"Can we have you miss Jade please"

My eyes fell on overly perky lady, "as cocky as you look I can already tell that I like you, though your face scream mean but your rosy cheeks and the sparkle in your pretty eyes his a sense of innocence to you that balance it out.

Another pair of eyes welcomed me, the one is serious expectant, a bald , overweight man with thick glasses, but his skin dripping wealth,and his looks telling intelligence.

Miss we are still waiting for you a familiar voice called out.

" o sweet Jesus the voice matches the face, how can a

man be this perfect common I turned to take a proper look "now if this is Temisan Greg then I'm definitely going to faint"

I continued my debate and criticism in my thought my eye not leaving the un bordered Temi, Lord have I fainted?"" I screamed in my thought again as I drew a chair to seat my leg caught on the edge of it, I fell on my buttocks earning sneers from the two faces except for Temi who didn't have any emotions written on his,I sighed got up and dusted my skirt "great first impression Kiki, you're fitting right in".

" I'm sorry lady and gentle men" an embarrassing sound escaped my lips.

"Now that we have your attention can we meet you please"

"Can we meet you please wow Temi is asking to meet me, Okay my name is Jadesola Okikiola Johnson, CEO Jakijo investment" I said adjusting in my seat keeping a straight face "I'm definitely not going to put myself on the spot, I hope your selective amnesia remains permanent"

About four other board members joined us and I was asked to do my presentation.

The anxiety left immediately as I saw who I will never want to see me fail, I stood graciously walked to the screen delivering my presentation avoiding his look as much as I could, I wowed everyone as they were nodding affirmatively.

"Thank you so much everyone if there's no more question for me I beg to go back to my seat"

"There's no more question Miss Kiki, this is a brilliant idea" Mr Ken praised me adding more shoulder pads to the one I was already wearing in my imagination.

Thank you sir and to everyone " I bowed and walked back to my seat.

***

I slumped on the bed, confused, I reached out to my phone and dialed Toni

"I'm already at the reception, coming up to ask how the meeting went" she said at the other end of the phone.

"Omg are you a ghost or something, you keep appearing and disappearing"

"To the first question I am not a ghost and the second I don't know what something is"

A loud knock announced her arrival, I opened and she jumped in all smiley

"Whatup sis" she jumped on the bed

" I feel good parararammm" she sang excitedly

"What's going on"

She flashed her left finger for me to see the ring on her finger.

"Wow he proposed girl congratulations I'm happy for you guys, you both deserve the best"

"Yeah thanks babe I really love him and I know he loves me too"

"I know right he couldn't stop talking about you every time I called him from the State"

Wow I admired the diamond ring

"I came to take you out to celebrate with us since you prefer this hotel room to our small apartment"

"Is it that mansion you're calling small apartment, but you know this is free man, I can't waste the company money naw, plus you guys need space to bond"

"We have been bonding since, come and let's go celebrate with us jor"

"I wish I can go with you but I can't right now, my head is spinning and I need to rest"

"Haba why are you such a kill joy naw, did you go there to pound yam ni, which one is your head is pounding"

"Temi is one of those I will be be working with for the three months and his also our presidential candidate"

"Temisan Greg" Toni screamed

"One and only""

"Tell me you're kidding"

"I wish I am"

Aww babe"

"I know right this is the first time in years I really don't know what to do" I bowed my head feeling really confused.

"What do I do really?"

"Are you seriously asking me that question, what else will you do than to raise your head up high and be the strong woman you've always being, do the work you were born to do (touching lives) but wait why are you the one feeling bad when he was the one who choose another woman over you, or is t the fact that he might be the next president that's bordering you?"

"No not at all he might have done this to me but I know his not a bad person., he's the best person for the job"

"If you say so then it must really be the truth, so why don't you guys talk and find out from each other what really happened though"

"What do you mean find out what really happened we both know what happened naw, didn't I tell you the story"

"You did but according to what you told me, his mom was the one who told you he chose to marry some else because of his political career"

"And is that not enough truth?, she couldn't have lied?"

What if she did?" The sound of those letters from Toni's voice gave me a punch in my reflective sense

"But why didn't he look for me"

"You left almost immediately remember, but honestly if this is the truth then their family has really lost a chance to have a rare gem, a woman with a heart of gold beautiful in and out, an angel in human form"

Toni's praise got me emotional I broke down in tears

Common cheer up Jade and let's go and celebrate with us"

"I don't know men.."

"You know I won't take no for an answer naw if you're changing you better go and do it now or else"

"... I will drag you out in your pajamas" we both chorused and started laughing

Toni seriously thank you, you are always a darling what will I do without you"

"Nothing obviously"

They laughed again.

"Meet us at the reception and be fast oo" she said and left.

***

TEMI POV

I walked into the house like an armed robbery trying to avoid my mom knowing she must've called like a million times, my phone was on answering machine on purpose, because I couldn't get Sam's word of advise out of my head "...don't make someone joyful at your own detriment, don't marry someone because you don't want to hurt them, don't..."

The light turned on scaring the daylight out of me, standing in her glory is Margret Tasha herself the one whose order everyone in the family must obey.

"Why was your phone switched off"

"I didn't switch it off , I just put it on airplane mode because I was busy"

"What's the difference I wasn't able to reach you now was I?"

"I'm so sorry mom I was extremely busy"

"You've said that before , aren't you always busy, the bottom line is you disappointed me today again Temi, Val and her family were here for the dinner and introduction but you were no where to be found"

"Forgive me mom you know that it's just three months I have on this massive project, all hands must be on deck, so I was buried in work and totally forgot about dinner"

"You forgot Temi, why are you bent on shaming this family"

"I don't understand mom"

"You don't understand what"

"I don't understand how I'm shaming the family I have practically lived my life for, the family I have chosen it happiness over mine, the family I have obeyed all my life, no one has the right to say that to me especially not you mom" I stood up to my mom's wahala that I have been trying to avoid all these years, my voice burning with fury.

"Temi" she called out my name shocked at the sudden outburst.

"I cant believe that you're saying this to me when all I'm doing is help build your dream, how are you going to become what you want to become politically if you're not friends with those who know the way? Answer me young man" mom said her two hands hung on her waist ready for the arguments of the night.

"Mom I have my party already and the inauguration is this weekend so obviously I have friends and acquaintances already, look you can't continue to fix everything for everyone, let me do this alright, politics isn't a game its a call and only the caller can truly understand and run the course"

I said and walked away then halted without looking back "mom from now on, no one talks about getting married to anybody or tries to match make me with anyone, when I'm ready I will look for who to marry and get married please"

"That was my exact word to her this evening" dad said and walked up to where she was standing.

"That was your exact word, wow you amaze me Fred" my mom turned to him angrily.

"You amaze me Erica" dad fired back "I must confess how much I hate this part of you, treacherous and overbearing"

"So me trying to make our son a responsible man is treacherous and overbearing wow"

"Temi is a very responsible man even a blind person can see that, its just you trying to impose your decision on every one as usual and I don't know when marriage has become a yardstick for responsibility"

"Alright insult me all you want, all I know is I will keep doing what I feel is right for my children"

"You know this is not an insult, this is just me pointing out the truth" dad said again as my mom left him.coming towards the staircase, I quickly ran away from where I was eavesdropping into my room and turned the lock, removed my clothes and walked to the shower

All I need now is a hot bath,finish my gist with Sam, probably some tea and hit the bed.

"I'm tired of all of these really, how am I going to cope working with Kiki for three months just how" I complained to Sam over the phone.

"Why do I feel this is the right time for closure, I think you guys should talk"

"You think that's a good idea?"

"I don't think that's a good idea but what needs to be done bro" Sam said again she always knows what to do or say in every situation.

"Okay I guess I should just get it done and over with"

"That's the spirit bro, talk to our rich hanty (auntie)" they both laugh

"Where did she get all the money from though, she carries more than half of the share for the project mehn"

"See? You have many things to ask her"

"No way I'm not going to ask her that what f she thinks I'm warming up to her because she's now wealthy "

"Just joking you definitely can't ask her that, why do you think I didn't reach out to her when I head she came to the State so that it won't look like I'm trying to look for her cos of the money you know"

"Hmmm true but the girl is in money man*

" Yeah I heard it was a transfer of wealth"

"From who?"

"I heard was from her dad"

"Really she found her dad?"

"Well yes I didn't get the real gist but rumor has it that the man is dead"

"Alright now,good for her, so babe I have to go to bed now, a lot to do tomorrow and with our rich auntie, it's even gonna be more stressful"

"Aww bro I understand but I still think the best thing is to let it all out, just talk to her"

"I think it's a good idea too"

"Are you saying there's gonna be feed back when next I call"

"Sure sis you're right it's better talk to her"

"Awesome bro, so we'll talk soon yeah"

"Yeah take care, I love you"

"Love you too bye".

***

I was waiting for so long for a miracle to come

Everyone told me to be strong, hold on don't shed a tear

Through the darkness and good time

I knew I'd make it through uuh

And the world thought I had it all

But I was waiting for you

Hush now I see q light in the sky

Oh it almost blinding me

I can't believe I have been touched by an angel with love

Let the rain come down and wash away my fear

Let it shatter the wall for a new sun

Anew day has come....."

Kiki singing and Temi playing the guitar, just as they were about to kiss.

Temi jumped up from the dream land

"Of course l it has to be a dream" his face rumpled as he checked the bedside clock and it was reading 7am, he got up yarning, stretched a bit and hit the floor for his hundred press up routine before heading to the bathroom.

CHAPTER EIGHT

KIKI POV

How in heavens' name am I going to cope working in the same place with Temi for three months, where do I start from, which Karma am I paying for oh Lord. I entered and slumped sit on the chair backing the door, I turned to see who was knocking when Temi walked in with a stern look on his face and dropped a file on my table, rudely.

"Kiki this is the business plan you asked for yesterday, I want you to take a look at it and let me know if there's going to be any adjustment later"

"Miss Kiki please..." I corrected "..and you don't come in and drop stuff on people's table like that as if you're their boss, next time I'm going to have you return it and bring it back when you're in a better mood"

He starred at me in shock "yes boss" he let out mockingly

"I must confess that you've done so well for yourself" he added with a taunting smile and walked to the door.

"Of course God has been faithful"

He halted at the sound of that, turned and said "God" then walked to the door and slammed it after him

Wow I'm in for a big one, Temisan giving me attitude, when the idiot was the one that choose some unknown bitch over me.

***

TEMI POV

I felt like bouncing on her and straggling her to death, when she was flashing that overconfident, I don't care what you think of me smile, so full of herself, no aorta of remorse or regret in the way she looked back there at the board room, when she saw me yesterday and earlier today in her office oh my God but why am I still feeling this way about her, please Lord help me.

I will go right away and put an end to this rubbish.

I met her at the hall way almost at my office door

"I see you've closed for the day" I said trying hard to maintain my cool.

"Yeah, I was coming to drop this on your table, I made some adjustment, we'd discuss it tomorrow"

"Can we talk now please"

I just said we'll talk tomorrow "

"Not work related"

"Well what could this be about?" She said in an annoying tone

"Don't you think we really need to talk?"

"What about Dr Temisan, if this is not work related then I don't think I have time to discuss anything with you, have a good evening" she turned to leave, I grabbed her by the arm and pulled her along into my office.

"What is this" she said her voice burning with fury.

" We are having this conversation and it's right now Kiki"

"Okay I'm listening" she folded her arms on her chest obviously trying hard to be calm also

"Good I have been praying for this day to come when I will be able to stand face to face with you and ask how it was convenient for you to choose money over our love"

"Money? What money are you talking about?"

"Don't give me that nonsense pretentious look, mom told me everything"

"Mom told you what"

"You know you should be an actor you act so well Kiki, I'm through with you, you can go now"

"Go where, you do not get to talk to me anyhow you like Mr Man, I don't know what money you're talking about"

She paused for awhile then "oh did she tell you that I collected money from her"

"Well did you not"

"Oh well I didn't, I will never collect anything from a woman like your mother even it were my ticket to heaven"

"Are you saying my mom is lying"

"She might not be lying per se but it's obvious she hasn't been truthful either because she told me you choose to marry one Val or vin whatever because of your political career, so why don't you get home and ask your dear mom the truth teller" she said making her way out of my office.

"You're got to be kidding me" I said under my breath.

"Kiki please wait up" I grabbed her , she flipped the arm and stepped a way from my reach.

"Don't touch me and please stay far away from me except any work related stuff don't dare come near me, I hope we're clear, have a good evening" she said and stormed out.

I got home very late and furious, I went straight to mom and dad's room.

I knocked severally before a groan answered me at the back of the door, I let myself in, though it was late I couldn't wait till morning to point mom's sin to her face.

I met only her on the bed as I switched on the light.

"Where's dad?"

"I thought he told you he was going for Chief Dare's burial" she replied sleepily.

"Okay good, awesome timing I need to talk to you mom"

"Let's wait till tomorrow, I'm really tired Temi, do you know what time it is though" she said in a whisper

"It can't wait till tomorrow, I want to talk to you right now"

She rolled on her shoulder at the sound of my demanding tone

"Okay what is it?"

"Why did you lie to me that Kiki collected money from you to leave me alone and also told her that I choose Val because of my political career"

Her sleepy eyes quickly turned to a stare as she sat up looking like a local third that had just been caught.

"I errr.." She stuttered for words.

"But mom how is running people's lives so convenient for you though"

"Shut up, don't insult me young man, I was just trying to help you get to your dream in the shortest possible way"

"Wow how ironic, if you must know mom, Kiki is the

chairperson for DPP, she has the power to appoint and terminate appointment"

"What, same Kiki"

"Yes mom the very same Kiki, you see how bitchy karma can be right, have a goodnight" I left her mouth agape and stormed out banging the door after me in annoyance.

***

KIKI POV

I couldn't afford to stay at the hotel room alone, so I headed to Lix and Toni's, I broke down in tears trying to explain everything to them.

They comforted me as usual and Toni suggested I checked out of the hotel and come to stay with them for the period that I will be in Nigeria, I agreed and promised to get my stuff the next day to come after work.

Just as I was coming out of the elevator when I stopped by in the morning to have a change of cloth, I saw someone in front of the door, I walked to the person as I received the shock of my life Temi slept in front of my hotel room.

"What are you doing here" I asked angrily

"Kiki please forgive me"" he said on his knees

"Temi get up and stop embarrassing yourself I had forgiven a long time ago"

"Then can I have my love back"

"Which love, please leave my door let me go in and change and I also suggest you start heading home now to freshen up , I'm sure you still remember that the partners are coming for 10, this is already 8:30"

"Alright" he stood and turned as if he was leaving then pushed me and jumped in with me as soon as I opened the door

" Can't you see Mom played us both, she broke us up"

"Yes she did a great job because I'm so over you,am I really over you can I be over be over you I said in my thought

" Well maybe you will have to teach me how to be over you"

He said and grabbed me, pinned my two hands up over my head and started browsing my mouth with his tongue. Oh God my whole body went numb.

When he released me from his grip, I slapped him and was about to walk away, he grabbed me again and gave me another passionate kiss that rendered me breathless.

Still holding me in a tight embrace he looked into my eyes and said "Look straight into my eyes and tell me you don't feel anything for me any more and I will go out of that door and never bother you again"

"I err" was the only thing that came out of my mouth at that moment, my throat went dry at thought of having to go another day without him.

I thought so too" he said, kissed me and walked to the door, before let himself out he said again " you will be seeing me every where close you from now on, I'm never gonna let you go again" he let himself out.

I sat on the bed touching my lips still feeling his own over mine he still has so much effect on me after so many years.

***

I got to the office before the meeting after the whole drama, I walked the hall way silently praying in my heart that Temi will not see me because I didn't know how to behave around him after this years, I still love him very much but I want to give him a tough time before I let it down again, I don't want to be seen as weak but truth be told I realized that Temisan was my weakness.

I stepped into the office and met some beautiful bunch of roses and a card, I groaned against the card that I have read like a million time when a knock on then door brought me back to my senses.

Temi came in looking all smashing in his blue suit and white shirt with a matching tie, "oh mine" I screamed in my thought staring at him.

"What are you doing here" I let out to cover my shameful act.

"Good morning to you too love of my life"

"Temi what do you want"

"Did you know that the meeting with the partners has been rescheduled to 2pm"

"Yes I have a PA"

"Okay I forgot, anyways that's not even why I'm here"

"Yes why are you here?"

"First of I will like to remind you that you're going to be seeing me often because I can not afford to lose you again and secondly the inaugural dinner party with Mr Ken and all the party members is tomorrow"

"I'm the chairperson that's if you still remember"

"Alright alright I just wanted to be your PA now that I know I'm bad at it can I ask if you will be kind enough to he my plus one?"

"I have a date already"

Temisan's s smile disappeared, he looked like a lion that has just lost his prey

"Yeah that's the idea you don't have to get me back easily" I smirked in my thought

"Someone I know?" He asked in a depressing tone.

"I don't think is any of your business though but for courtesy sake, it isn't someone you know we just met not long ago and I'd prefer you stay away from us thank you"

I will advice you tell him not come I won't be staying away KIKI you know I won't, I have made that mistake of staying away for a long time not any more "

"I'm in a relationship Temi don't come and spoil it for me" I said looking serious.

"I don't see any wedding band on your finger that means it isn't serious yet" he smiled, crossed over to my chair lean down and kissed my neck held my face to his and said

" I will never let you go again Kiki, not again, so be prepared for a show if you bring another man to the dinner tomorrow " he walked confidently to the door and turned back "don't say I didn't warn you" he left.

Strangely I love the tone and also the threat itself.

***

I entered the dinner very late, yes it was intentional just because of Temi

I didn't bring the date because I looked for and didn't see, Lix was out of it because he had to go to see Toni's parents over the weekend and I have left the country for a while couldn't even remember any of my friends that could fit in.

"Good girl I'm glad you didn't dare me" he walked up to me and tried to take my hand, I stepped away from his reach.

I didn't bring him because he has to be somewhere urgently " I said hastily as my words betrayed me

"He should just remain there and never come back and what took you so long, are you avoiding me?"

"Get over yourself Temi, avoid you for what, like I don't know this is as important to me as it is to you"

I left him drooling over me as I went to join Mr Ken and Co at the VIP table.

After my address I excused myself to a corner of the hall and sat quietly where I could probably have a proper view of the most handsome man in the room before I could relax my head he was there beside me and I l almost screamed

" What is it Temi, what do you want from me"

"You know what I want tell me you've forgiven me" he said with a serious look

"Okay I have forgiven you, can I enjoy the dinner in peace now"

"Yes you can only if you assure me that I can have my heart back"

"Who removed your heart"

"You Kiki you" he drew close to me his face close to mine we had a moment then started kissing I forgot where I was just buried in the moment

"I love you so much Kiki" he groan against my mouth though I didn't say any thing but my heart altered many words.

Tell me you still love me Kiki please, I need that assurance baby,I'm going crazy"

"You hurt me Temi you didn't look for me ,you and Sam abandoned me when I needed you guys the most you left me"

"Belief me I did before I left for the state, I searched every where for you, I was told you moved out , I was depressed for many years I didn't know why you would choose money over our love"

"I didn't and I will never I loved you"

"And why is the love in past tense , you still love me Kiki don't you.,please say yes" he searched my eyes for answer

"Yes" I let out hastily disappointed in my self

A sweet smile pasted on his cute face as he lean excitedly and kissed me again.

I love you so much and I'm sorry again" he said and left then came back a moment later with his two sisters.

"Omg who do we have here" Tee baby said as they both jumped on me.

"Kiki we are sorry"

"Hey guys" I said shutting them up, it's alright we are good now there's no need to be sorry anymore,I'm sure our been apart for awhile is just something that couldn't be erased from our love story, I knew when I was living that if he was for me we would find his way back to each other,look now we are back together I love your brother very much and nothing can keep us apart any more I promise"

Temi looked from me to his sisters true happiness boldly written on his face as we all did a group hug.

Adenike Isenibi

CHAPTER NINE

TEMI POV

I heard a loud knock on my door , I grumbled and got out of bed before I could reach it my Margaret Tacha had let herself in

"Mom this is a man's room who is not your husband, when you knock you let him ask you in before you open the door"

"Are you okay?" She said looking like she was ready to make her usual trouble, Ignored the look on her face.

"Good morning to you too mom, to whom do I owe this early morning visit?"

"When were you planning on telling me this?" She threw the celebrity in and out magazine at me

Okikiolamihan Jadesola Johnson Was sighted at the inaugural dinner of DDP with the presidential aspirant Dr Temisan Greg Lewis in a love tango, rumor has it that those two have history together and it seems there's going to be rekindling of lost fire of love, our fingers are crossed.

"Oh that, yeah I was going to give you this yesterday" I checked my bedside drawer for a note pad wrote Kiki's address and phone number on it and handed it over to her

"What is this?" She collected, read and frowned her face.

"Yeah mom that's Kiki's address and phone number, you're going to go there and apologize to her because this is happening and it's very soon mom" I said as I waved the magazine at her to complete my statement

"What! I can't go there, I won't"

"I won't argue with me if I were you"

"But what do I tell her" mom said childishly looking seriously disturbed.

"I don't know mom just apologize and make sure she accepts your apology that's all"

I left her there and jumped into the bathroom humming out loud.

***

KIKI POV

I rushed out of the bathroom to pick my phone that won't stop ringing.

"How are you doing dear" I heard a familiar voice.

"I'm doing great may I know who this is please?"

"She has even forgotten my voice, okay my name is Samantha Onabanjo Durojaiye" Same said at the other end of the phone.

"Omg Sam I just wanted to be sure it's you"

"Yes it's me your former best friend"

"You know you're always my best friend the place has been vacant since you left me"

"Since you left me you mean to say"

"Omg I've missed you so much"

"That's an understatement for me Kiki, I was shattered, I was heartbroken and disappointed, why did you leave like that without telling me anything"

"I'm sorry Sam I had to leave, I didn't want to be near anything that would remind me of Temi"

"But you could've talked to me first" Sam said

"I'm so sorry dear, I made a terrible mistake should've let you know where I was going to"

It's alright babe how are you?, Temi has gisted me about you, him and mom escapade"

"Yes o babe serious matter I tell you"

"So what's up everything cool now I mean between you and my Cousin"

"Yes babe I still love him very much"

"Hmmm" Sam breath against the phone "thank God"

"Yes babe so how is Timi and my boy eerrr

" which your boy er" she said sarcastically "godmother that doesn't know the name of her godson"

" What I'm his godmother "

"Yeah and Temi is his godfather"

"Wow are you serious, did you know were going to come back together some day?

"Yeah of course I asked God everyday to help me fix it

between you guys, Temi was depressed just buried in his work no social life since you left"

"Omg" I said tears rushing down my face

" I'm glad God finally answered my prayer this is a miracle, I will be eternally be grateful to him" Sam sniffed I could sense that she was shedding tears of joy too.

"God is faithful babe, aww I'm coming to yours for my many years of missed gists"

Hun which gist do I have compared to yours Kiki, I'm so not breathing a word until I hear all your own, me that have heard that you're the richest Hanty (auntie) in the world right now"

"Which richest aunty"

"You know that you can't play that humble thing with right"

"Okay okay I hear you"

We both laughed again

"So when are we hearing the wedding bell"

"That question is for your brother o babe"

"You know he will jump and do it today if you want it"

"Okay I will go and propose to him tomorrow"

"Aww Kiki will never change, you know that's not what I'm saying naw, She said amidst laughter.

" Okay" I said lightly as we both laughed out loud against our phones. A persistent knock cut short our reunion gist.

"Orekelewa let me call you back someone is at the door"

"Alright hon"

I ended the call and walked to the door, opened it and staring at Temi's mom

I stepped out of the door at the sound of "won't you allow me in"

"Come in ma'am"

She walked in as I closed the door turned to see her on her knees I rushed towards her and helped.her up

"Please. Don't do that ma'am"

"Please forgive me Kiki"

"I have forgiven you ma'am"

"Are you sure?"

"Very sure ma'am I said with a genuine smile

She embraced me " thank you my love she said in total repentance

"You're welcome ma'am"

So now that we're friends I'd love us to do lunch tomorrow, if that's okay by you of course"

"Okay ma"

Thank you so much, I will text you the address take are of yourself for me alright see you tomorrow" she left.

Adenike Isenibi

CHAPTER TEN

KIKI POV

I got like three outfits for the date with Temi's mom and I didn't end up with any of them.

I settled for a simple gown, my heart beating fast as I made my way to the reservation table, she was sitting on waiting

"Oh I'm sorry hope you haven't been waiting for too long ma'am" I apologized , drew out a chair and sit

"It's fine Kiki, I don't you think it's high time you started calling me mom"

"Oh mom" I said shyly

A waiter came in took our order and fifteen minutes later our table was filled with variety of food

We started eating, I was beginning to relax and enjoying myself, when suddenly, the music changed to our song "A New Day Has Come" then I began to see Temi's friends and sisters matching in, all wearing white T. Shirt. When they were fully in, they turned their back at us, and then I saw the letters that read."KIKI, WILL YOU MARRY" I was shocked. The letters did not make a complete proposal and I am yet to see who was making the proposal. Then I felt a hand on shoulder, when I turned, I saw Temi on his knees with his customised shirt that completed the proposal. I was overwhelmed with joy. I covered my wet face and exclaimed Yes Yes Yes babie I will marry you!!………………………………………

My dad didn't show up, thank goodness!! I expected that so I was not too surprise about it and my mum kept her usual straight face, no smile, in fact no show of any kind of emotion.

Even when it was time for the Bride parents to pray for the couple. I could hear the voice of Uncle Ambrose as loud as the man using the microphone, but mum's mouth was "sealed" the only thing I saw was her right hand stretched towards us.

What could possibly be the matter with you? Mom I thought

Is it the death of Olamiposi or because dad left or is it both? It's been nine years now mom, don't I deserve to be at least one of the reasons for your happiness? A reason for you to look to the sky and say thank you Lord.

I guess you will never get out of this web of sadness you have kept yourself in all these years, not even the wedding of your daughter your only child can make you smile.

You suddenly stopped caring about me nine years ago so why am I even bothering myself over you now

Well good luck to you mother sadist. I almost hissed.

It happened like the fairy tale wedding, like prince charming and Cinderella. Our marriage ceremony was superb; thumbs up to Crown's innovative skills, our wedding planner. OMG!! He did a great job.

I didn't want it to end; it wasn't such a bad idea after all.

When grandma insisted I have my wedding at the village, I got mad but couldn't say no to her, Crown told me "it's ok Kiki you don't have to cry, I will make your wedding the most talked about in that village, trust me"

He did more than what he had promised.

You can't blame me, the thought of having to put up with those village gossips for five days and not having my Samantha there with me got my head aching.

"Oh gurl you don't know how much I'm missing you here" I told her when she called

"I am freaking out here mehn" I continued, folding on the small bed, you know me and village stuff babes, after listening to my outpour on the phone, she agreed with me about not been in with village stuff either and then counselled me as always .

"Gurl just keep your head up, smile when you can, greet when you can, don't eat their food or drink their water except your grandma's ok"

"Ok babe'

"Then promise me you are not going to allow this, ruin your day"

"I promise babe" I muttered babyishly.

"Ok babes have the most wonderful wedding and I pray you will live happily ever after"

"Amennnnnn" I said

"Can't wait to have you guys join us here in the state"

"Can't wait too dearie" I replied excitedly

"I love you Kiki"

"Love you too Sam"

"Bye babes"

"Bye!"

***

"Well well well, here we are" Temi said as we were entering one of the biggest houses they have in Abuja.

Everybody was seated in the living room to receive us, his mum, dad, and his two beautiful sisters.

"Look who we have here the great Mrs Greg Jnr in her splendour and majesty' his dad announced and they all rushed to the door to give me a warm welcome

I was blushing with joy "oh what a lovely family" I was given a special treatment

"Sweetheart, you are welcome officially to this great family" my mother in law said

"I want you to know that you are one of my daughters now; I am not taking you as my daughter in law……."

"Yes and as our sister too" Tee baby the last baby of the family interrupted

"Thank you so much ma, am glad to be part of this beautiful family" I said shyly.

"We all love you" Tare and daddy chorused

"I love you people too"

We hugged, had dinner together and everybody rushed to their rooms to pack up for their journey the next day.

I and Temisan have two more days to spend in Nigeria before we finally leave for the state.

CHAPTER
ELEVEN

I must have slept for a very long time, the very first day after I was turned to a woman, I felt great, and the room was filled with the bright sunlight of the early afternoon.

The fresh manly smell of my husband spread all over the room, hmmmm my husband the thought of that gave me a rush in my spine, I opened my eyes and closed them back again.

Temi stood across the bed and whispered "morning sun shine" my eyes flew open, "have you been here all the while?" I felt embarrassed

"Yes my love" he crawled in bed with me and grabbed

me with his two hands, "I have been watching this pretty face smile in her sleep"

"You are so beautiful Kiki" he pulled me to him "you are the best thing that has ever happened to me"

"I love you so much"

"Oh baby" I am blushing I playfully held my checks in both hands, "I love you even more" I whispered to him.

"Jeez baby why didn't you wake me up, its 12:30" as my eyes travelled to the wall clock I disengaged from him

"I thought your people's flight was for 11?"

"Yeah they have gone" he said "smile-frowning"

"What! oooo no naw, you would have woken me up"

"To do what baby? Drive them to the airport?" he asked laughing at me

"Lemme alone, not that jor, at least prepare breakfast for them and bid them good bye, silly" I said and threw one the pillows at him.

"Was gonna wake you up though but mom said No, that you must really be very tried, the stress, the dance and all" he winked at me

"Even at that haba baby"

"it's aii" he closed the gap between us and swept me into his hands

"Now get your pretty self out of that bed and let's go get something to eat"

"I made us breakfast" he said proudly as he placed me on one of the dinning chair.

"Wow seriously"

"Yes Mrs Greg seriously, he said humorously trust me, you gonna bite your tongue if you are not careful"

Let's wait and see Doctor chef I said amidst laughter

He made fried rice, pepper sauce chicken and coslaw

"Wow when did you make all of these?" I asked in amazement.

"I made it When my wife was busy smiling in her sleep and since then been praying for her to wake up now let's just say we having our brunch and all thanks to you, wifey". He eyed me.

"Yes o that's what a husband gets when he over pampers his wife" I said with a loud laugh.

"Whatever mehn" he gave me "talk to the hand".

Oh Lord thank you for this meal and the privilege to eat together as a family, thank you for giving me such a pretty and intelligent wife, thank you Lord for what you are doing and about to do (amen)

"Amen".

"You can always be a chef if you get tired of being a medical doctor baby" I joked later

"This is just a perfect way to have our first breakfast as a family my love, this food is heavenly hmmmm"

"I won't be tired of being a medical doctor he said just like I won't be ever tired of loving and spoiling my beautiful wifey"

I looked at him and smiled warmly

He smiled back and exclaimed "I'm glad wifey likes my delicacy"

"We are going out today to collect the things Sam's mom wants to send to her, visit some nice places and have our dinner somewhere special and it's a surprise so don't even ask me where he waved his hands to warn me, and then we are back home to prepare for tomorrow's journey"

"Yes your highness" I said mockingly

We settled for our customised tee shirt and blue jeans.

"Babie he held me suddenly I don't mean to spoil this

fun or make you upset. But please I seriously think we should see your mom before we travel tomorrow"

"I don't want to see her baby please, I mean when will I stop pushing myself on her, it's obvious she doesn't care if we talk to each other or not"

"No babes can't you see she is not happy, can't you see pain written all over her, I felt so uncomfortable at our wedding I had an eye contact with her and saw those eye balls begging for mercy" plus remember what our youth pastor will tell us, "be kind to those who don't even deserve it"

"Look you don't have to say anything, let's just go there and say hi, let her know you care despite all"

"Pleassssseeee love"

"Ok I will try"

"That's my babie" he said and gave me a kiss.

Adenike Isenibi

CHAPTER TWELVE

KIKI POV

Should I just use this table knife, I thought pushing at the table with clenched fist.

I reached out to where the electric kettle was boiling the water with bubbles making a disturbing noise, the bubbles dancing inside the kettle reminding me of a well-timed pouring of that water on his face might be the easier way to dispatch Temisan Greg or should I just get a fast poison to put in his favourite African white soup like the kind he had on Friday night before rushing out to catch his flight to Paris for his supposedly Medical Association of United state Annual meeting.

I found a white small paper with a woman's lipstick at the back in the pocket of the suit jacket he had asked me to dry clean for him. I opened it and saw an address written in a small paper, I could picture the sinner's lips saying I deliver this to you with a kiss.

That announced his infidelity as loud as the headline news at the front page of the daily newspaper.

"I could shoot him" I thought squeezing the life out of the sliced bread I placed on a saucer for my tea, as if I was squeezing the trigger of a gun.

My eyes following the imaginary bullet as it's passing across the dinning towards my husband's heart as he rose to give his presentation at MAU annual meeting.

I watched him unbutton his grey jacket just seconds before the bullet ripped through it, the boyish little half smile that emanated as much from his eyes as his lips, freezing, fading then disappearing altogether as he fell, face down to the hard floor of the large room made partly of glass.

Death to the infidel I shouted, kicking at the table as if trying to escape from a small tight cell, my legs feeling unexpectedly heavy. For some minutes I felt my legs were foreign objects, as if they belong to someone else, my stomach tightened as I staggered up the chair and gboaaa! the sound of my right ankle on the dining table, I muttered through a painful groan, splash of tea all over my green and white striped shirt. "Serves me right for having such an evil thought" I said to myself.

I grabbed one of my kitchen napkins to clean the messy table, and then burst into a painful cry with hot tears flowing down my face.

OMG!! I can't believe this; I held my aching head with my right hand.

I can't believe in my wildest imagination that Temi could do this to me

O God not again, wake me up from this terrible night mare please God please.

"Kiki! Kiki!! Kiki!!! we will be late gurl"

Samantha Durojaiye ran into the Kitchen, "come on you are leading the choir ministration now remember, we should not be late"

She had come to spend the weekend with me; Timi has taken their children for a weekend holiday at the Bahamas

"Oooh don't tell me you are still giving a treat to that endowed voice of yours" she teased

"Jeez babe!! Sup with you? Are you ok?"

She said when I finally turned to face her, I opened my mouth but could not say anything, I just focused on Sam like a movie at the cinema.

She rushed forward and held me to herself, "it's ok babe it's ok" she patted me at the back.

Still holding me she asked again

"What is it Kiki?"

"I'm fine Orekelewa" I teased her because I didn't know if I was ready to tell her or not

"No No No, babe" she protested, "I won't buy that at all"

"Tell me why I'm seeing this stream of water fall on your face"

"Ok Sam I will be good, why don't we rush off to church and I'd tell you everything after the service, besides we have plans of picking Alex together and then straight to your house for our Sunday coffee isn't it?" I said wiping the tears on my face with the back of my hand

"Ok o" Sam agreed reluctantly dragging me along with her to the living room

"Here, seat let me make you up, we have just ten minutes to rush down to church"

I had a quick make over and Sam took the steering of my Bentley Temi got me as a surprise birthday gift.

***

"Excuse us please" I said as we made our way to the choir stand,

"Sorry please"

Samantha found herself a seat, "please excuse me" I repeated to Deacon Maryann an elderly woman in her mid-sixties, she is the head of the church holy gossips, these people are unique backbiters, they know the story about everything and everyone, "now what the hell is she doing at the back row she has never come late for any church service, help me Lord to be able to put up with her till the end of this service" I released the breath I have been holding since I sighted her near the only available seat.

I squeezed myself in the middle of the seventh and last row of the choir's seat of the Church of Christ ministries and then I said yet again "excuse please" to the only soprano male singer I will be sitting beside for the better part of the morning.

I stepped into the choir robe and began to fumble with the zip.

"Let me help you with that" Deacon Maryann volunteered tugging at the stubborn zip before I had time to object, smiling at me, "thank you" I flashed her back a smile, but she had already turned twisting her neck with her shoulder raised high as always staring at the altar making her usual noise "halleluyah!"

"Amen"

"I'm glad to be here"

"Thank you Jesus".

Holding my breath, straightened the folds of my purple and lilac choir robe and making my way to the lead microphone

If this is your power, I could hear the melody of the song giving me a "delicious feedback"

"If this is your presence hmmmmmm

If this is your glory yeeeeh

So let it rain"

Choir help me sing

Choir repeated

"Wow that was wonderful sister Kiki, you are simply an angel dropped in our choir by God" comes the strong deep voice of the choir coordinator.

"Glory to God" I replied as I playfully straighten my neck and my two hands raised high

"Halleluyah" chorused Samantha and Auntie Bibi

"Ooooooh auntie Bibi thanks so much for helping me with Alex since Friday, I tell you, it's a real hard work and you don't know how happy I am, I had a lot of time to rest" I said and gave her a hug

"Always sweetheart, your boy is the most brilliant chap I have ever met" she said with a sincere smile.

"Thank you auntie"

"Yeah dearie you are welcome"

"Look I have to go now"

"Auntie Bibi not even our usual Sunday coffee together, why the rush"

"My love I have to see a client, right now there's a project I am working on, Alex is in the children church dear" she said not looking back from her slow run

"Alright auntie, odabo ma, ma call yin"

"Ok odabo"

'Mummy! Mummy!" I turned at the sound of my six years old son's voice, running out of the children's department of the church with so much excitement written over his cute face.

"Here you are, handsome!" I squatted to receive him in my opened arms; he tightened his hands around my neck and gave me a kiss.

"Hello auntie Samantha" he said almost screaming

"Hey little spiderman" Sam gave him a hand shake "how was your weekend with mummy Bibi?"

"twas great aunt Sam"

Alex plumb, very handsome and highly intelligent , I know the line and well placed structure of my son's face, just like his father's maybe better, yea, better.

"I saw you and Aunt Sam running into the church when I was about to enter the children church, were you guys late for your choir again mum" he made a face at me.

I playfully pulled his ear and said "look at your small mouth"

"Yea son, my alarm officer was away on a whole full weekend tour with his Granny Bibi so what do you expect?" I bent down to answer him, "mum over slept" rolling my eyes

Alex giggled at my face and I gave my hand to my happy son to hold as we made our way towards the parking lot

Alex has been another great source of joy to Temi and I, I can see it written all over him, every time he is with us is always a memorable one, especially when it has anything to do with his son he goes an extra mile.

"Mom when I grow up, I am going to buy us a Jet and pilot us, you, daddy and my little baby when she is born," hmm the swelling in my throat came again as I rubbed my swollen tummy "two more months to go thank you Jesus" I thought to myself"

"Even though you have decided to be a traitor Temi, I will always have my children here to love and care for"

"I will pilot us" the sound of Alex's tender voice brought me back to life

"Yeah honey" I said to him

"Yeah mom, I will pilot us round the world"

"I will take you guys to see the queen of England, Barrack Obama and ermmm just everywhere cool and interesting mum"

"Ahaaaa that's what I'm talking about my boy, thank you darling, I can't wait my prince"

"Ok oooo it's like my boyfriend has forgotten his girl friend auntie Samantha" Sam said hugging herself and making a face at Alex

"Of course not Aunt Sam, I will take you, Simisola, Folaranmi, Uncle Timi, my Grams Bibi and her nice friend"

"Ooh ok you met mummy Bibi's friend over the weekend yea"

"Yes mom and she somehow looks like you" he said.

"Wow really?" We chorused and laughed

"My mummy Bibi and her friend said I'm gonna be a cool pilot"

"Uhmm who is this Mummy Bibi's friend, that is so nice to my son and looks somehow like me o" I said smiling to Sam.

"We went to the zoo, the amusement park and to her shop together, she allowed me to sell a bag to one woman, I collected the money and counted it mum" Alex added proudly

"Wow! my boy is such a brilliant chap", I said turning my neck to look back at him from the passenger seat, "so how much did you sell the bag?" Sam added

"Ermmm, I think its errm 100 dollars" he said squeezing his face no it's 150"

"Ok I can't remember Auntie Sam" he said sadly and threw his hands up in surrendering

Sam glanced at me and we chuckled, "oh Alex that's ok, you don't have to be sad, we will have to ask your mommy Bibi later alright" Sam said hypocritically

"Alllllright .."

"Ok son we will be driving straight to auntie Sam's. What do you say?"

"Yeah mom, that will be cool, but only if Fola and Simi

are back I don't wanna watch cartoon or play games all by myself"

"You don't have any problem sweetie; they are back already" Sam said to him.

"Yepie! He exclaimed".

"yeah, they got back few minutes ago we'll meet them up at home ok" Sam added to his happiness

"Alright" Alex said with his eyes glowing with joy.

Folaranmi is Samantha's son who is a year and half older than Alex, he has a little sister Simi who is 5 years old, the three of them have built a very close relationship just like their fathers and mothers as little as they are.

Adenike Isenibi

CHAPTER THIRTEEN

Sam and I settled down in the garden with a bowl of pepper soup prepared by Troy the coolest chef as Timi would say.

Sam looked at me intently and said "please Kiki tell me what the problem is, I know you are not happy, I can see it in your eyes, I could see you trying to fight back the tears when we were driving down here, what is it darling let me share it with you" she took my hands in hers.

"Sam I think Temi is cheating on me, babe I can't take another heartbreak from any man, my dad broke my heart so badly, it took me so many years to be convinced that all men are not the same and now Temi, I think am going to die.

Should I say I was right or wrong, when I said men are bastards look at the way you pressured me to give my heart again, to learn to trust men"

"What! Sam exclaimed and threw my hands away, no way! Awwww Lord Jesus Kiki has started again", she said looking at the sky as if God just showed his face

You have started again, what is your problem huh, why does it have to be like "watch your back thing when it comes to men issue in your life? Why Kiki why?"

"Babe, here take a look at this, it's the note I got from his jacket few days ago"

"Huh! Really! Wow!

But are you sure this is real?" she said shaking her head

"Why? I don't get, what more prove do you want babe? Ooh yeah! I get you, you want to take sides with your cousin yeah"

"Cool babe, it's really cool" I stood to leave

Sam held me back and said "babe chill come on, you know I won't even choose my own mother over you"

"I mean" Sam said and held my face into her palms . "why would he be cheating on you and bring it right to your face Kiki, think about it?, Temi's love for you is indescribable plus he is a minister, I don't believe he can do something like this to you and will be bold enough to bring it to your face, if you will please calm down and let's look into this carefully"

I finally settled back on the chair, she handed me a cup of coffee

"Thank you babe" I said some few minute later, when all my nerves were fully relaxed, "you are a darling"

"I know" she said rolling her eyes

"So are you trying to say Temisan isn't cheating on me?" I asked

"Exactly babe, I just have this strong feeling that someone somewhere is trying to set him up to get his attention, maybe he has refused to give the harlot attention or something you know. Because I don't know the reason why he might want to keep such note in his pocket, when he knows that you will be the one doing the laundry, I don't know if this is making any sense, I might be wrong babe, but just give this a close look and see alright"

I nodded and said "I think he is, Sam, the sudden attachment to his phone, rushing out even on Saturdays when we are supposed to be together"

"I think he is having an affair Sam, I can feel it…….." I broke down in tears.

She drew me to herself

"But why Kiki?" Sam sounded dejected, "I think the Devil is at work here……….

But babe, I think you should confront him or do you want me to?"

"No no babe I will do it, but not now"

Not now? When babe? You guys are very close, do you think you will be able to pretend this had not happened

"I am not going to pretend Sam" I said gazing at the Statue opposite me

"Okay so what do you want to do then?"

"Don't worry dear I will handle it my own way, just please don't tell him anything yet, when I am through with what I think I should do, I will let you know, is that ok?

"It's ok" Samantha agreed reluctantly. "But hey babe in anything you are planning to do just be very careful, always bear it in mind that women build their homes, I will be praying for you guys dearie, the Devil is a liar."

After a long talk with Samantha I drove home with Alex laid on the back seat already fast asleep, I parked in the lot carried my boy carefully in to his room, changed him into his pyjamas and laid him on his bed.

I went quickly to my bedroom, couldn't wait to sleep and be out of the reality of this world for some hours, changed my cotton and striped shirt, slipped into a pink night gown and laid on the bed

My aching head had barely touched the pillow when my phone rang; I traced the bed side table without opening my eyes

"Hello" I said in a low tone as I press the receive button

"Hey babe" the warm affectionate voice of Temisan announced itself at the other end.

"I'm fine, thank you" I said almost getting irritated

"What's happening?"

"Nothing, the normal stuff" I answered sharply and frowned

"How is my boy? Sleeping already yeah?"

"Yeah"

"Sorry darling I didn't call all afternoon because I had an emergency, I couldn't even go to church"

How will you be able to go to church when your woman sinner mate is there with you giving you the sermon you need

"It's okay"

I could almost see his eye balls coming out of the sockets as he screamed back, "it's okay?"

"What is wrong babe?" He asked in a serious tone

"Nothing is wrong" I answered lightly

"You are beginning to make me feel uncomfortable and nervous, Kiki"

When he calls my name like that I know something is eating him up, yeah cool

"And I want you to know I am not appreciating this feeling at all; you have never acted this way with me before. I noticed you didn't call me throughout Saturday, I called three times and it has always been this cold tone, what have I done wrong?"

Yeah adulterer, pretender, bastard, who the hell cares about what you are feeling right now, I thought furiously

But words didn't leave my mouth they remained stuck in my throat, I left the question hanging

"Hello Kiki are you still there?"

"Yes I am"

"Well that's great" he said, I could feel the anger in his tone already

"The reason I called is to let you know I won't be able to come back tomorrow as planned"

(Of course how will you be able to come back as

planned, oloshi, when your mistress still has another day of pleasure to share with you doctor adulterer)

"It's alright by me" puzzled by my own answer, I shot him another surprise

"Well, cool then, I will be coming first flight on Tuesday, goodnight" not waiting for me to answer he ended the call.

"Safe trip doctor Temisan the adulterer" I murmured against the sound of the phone.

My brain still racing as I closed my eyes to sleep, Gosh!!! Men "Temisan Greg you are a bastard" I said squeezing the duvet

Even if you want to leave, the door is wide opened, I will give you the divorce any time you want but before you come to that conclusion I will sure give you my own pay back bastard.

Why must it always be me all the time, don't I deserve to be happy? God why me?, Temi how could you be such a traitor, how can you pretend so well, as if he cares picking up his Devilish phone to call all the time (imbecile) mtcheww, I will make sure you pay for all the pain you have caused me Temi, I let out an aching groan.

Adenike Isenibi

CHAPTER
FOURTEEN

TEMI POV

I kept tossing and tossing on the bed.

"What could possibly be wrong with you Kiki, what is the problem with you or should I have just stayed back?"

I kept asking myself a lot of questions, I barely slept for two hours when the alarm clock in my hotel room started ringing, I reluctantly got up with a heavy eyes.

After the morning section of the MAUA meeting, I got a seat far away from my colleagues to figure out what could possibly be wrong with my wife. I was staring at my food,

"I love you so much Kiki I said to myself, but I can't

seem to figure out what I have done to make you are this angry with me, I can't," I buried I my head in both palms.

"A penny for your thought I was startled back to life with a female voice, the voice was familiar and soft,achingly feminine, I looked up to see Doctor Olu my high school sweetheart.

"Oh God" feeling the pounding in my head became louder, I muttered "why is she here now?"

"Are you alright?" She asked

I nodded and said nothing

Oluyemi Adebiyi reached out as if to touch me then stopped merely inches from my shoulder.

"Is there anything I can do?" She asked

I shook my head; I knew she was asking me what the hell happened back there, how can the almighty Temi not have the answer to the simple question asked by the gynaecologist (Doctor Andrew)

"Are you concentrating at all doctor Greg?" Dr Andrew had asked

"Are you alright?"

" I am ok sir; I mean I will be ok sir"

"Are you sure you don't want to talk about this" Doctor Olu pushed further.

"Having probs with your wife?" My head snapped up as if someone had yanked a fistful of my hair

"Jesus! Olu" I bounced on my feet, "don't tell me you ...."

"I didn't call her" Oluyemi interrupted him sharply, "I didn't, I mean I don't even have her number so just calm down"

I eyed her with disgust and breezed past her back to the meeting room.

Dr Oluyemi Adebiyi's head turned to one side, as she shrugged, I still love you and I can't seem to help myself, I don't just mind sharing you with your wife, just a little of you sweetheart, she whispered after me

"You must be dreaming Olu, I love my wife and nothing can change that" I said and continued walking back to the meeting hall

"I hope this girl has not called Kiki, I hope not, I hope not, God! if she did what the hell am I gonna do" I kept talking to himself.

"This meeting is taking like forever oh God, I really need to get out of here, I am so tired already, I need to get back home as fast as I can, I can't concentrate any more"

I was lost in thought as my colleagues started matching in from their break.

"Hey you, you didn't have lunch with us and you were barely concentrating in the morning session, you're not your normal self bro, any challenge?" Dr Jat said touching my shoulder

" Just a little fatigued, I will be aii bro thanks for asking"

"Alright doc be good" he strolled back to his seat.

***

A sigh of relief as I was matching to the Airport, it was more like: can you just please get this engine started already, I was quiet all through the journey, buried in my thought, *"I can't wait to see you my angel, I just hope it's not what I'm thinking because I won't be able to forgive myself if I ever hurt you and make you lose your trust in me."*

"Thanks goodness Brad has never disappointed me" I thought as we pulled the car at the parking lot in our big mansion at Allen avenue, "my driver of four years, I am so proud of you" I continued in my thought.

"Thank you so much Brad, you can get the bags out please"

"My pleasure sir" Brad said with a smile.

I proceeded to the door, my heart slamming against my chest as I pressed the door bell.

"Yeah who is it?"

"Coming"

She opened the door, kissed me dutifully and turned immediately to leave, I held and pulled her back to me.

"What is the problem Kiki, I couldn't concentrate for the whole day at the meeting, you didn't call and even when I did you weren't flowing with me, babe come' I made her sit on my lap in the living room, "Talk to me ,what have I done wrong please tell me"

"You haven't done anything Temi" she got up making her way to the kitchen

"Why don't you go and have a shower, eat and rest"

"For real?" I said furiously, standing on my feet

"You won't tell me what is wrong, yeah?"

"Nothing is wrong Temi" She said not looking back

"So you have been acting up for nothing?"

"Just leave me alone please"

"Ohk cool, you want to be left alone yeah, I will do just that" I got angry and ran up the stairs.

Adenike Isenibi

CHAPTER
FIFTEEN

KIKI POV

"Don't touch me" I said sitting up on the bed.

"What is your problem? Why are you being mean to me?"

"What have I done?"

"Why don't you ask yourself Temi, I took you for everything but a pretender, you are acting it so well, is it part of your profession? Jeeez!!"

"Ok I agree with you, I am a pretender, just tell me what this is all about"

"Well I am not just in the mood to ………"

The door to Alex's room made a loud noise interrupting us, we both got out of bed to see what was going on,

Alex was already walking towards our room scratching his left eyes and the right one half closed

"You ok little man?" Temi rushed towards him

"The beast was chasing me, dad can I come sleep in your room please?"

"Don't worry hon, I will sleep with you on your bed alright" I said jumping in the bed holding him tightly

Thank goodness, I found a means of escape, Temi's eye widened, before he could say anything, "Can you please help us put the light off on your way out? Thank you"

Temisan remained standing in the middle of the room, looking from Kiki to Alex, a stunned expression on his handsome face.

"I don't understand Kiki we were talking" he said running his fingers through his head.

"Shhhhh you don't want to wake him up, do you?" I said looking down at my son.

Temisan shook his head and left the room in anger.

My mouth curved in a smile, I meant it when I said I will pay you back in your own coin Temi, holding my son more tightly and slept off.

***

TEMI POV

Early in the morning the next day Samantha gave me a call

"Finally cousin where the hell did you put your phone" Samantha screamed at me on the phone, I have been calling you since morning, your answering machine has almost recorded a 100 messages from me

"Hey sis, so sorry I'm just coming out of the operation room. How are you, my guys and Timi?"

"We are doing great, I need to talk to you bro"

"Yea sis I have wanted coming to see you too, I have just been very busy"

"Alright that makes the two of us"

"Ok Temi, can we do lunch today at Kim's"

"Alright babes"

"Ok, see you then "

"Great" I said and ended the call

***

Sam waved her hands to show me the Table she was sitting, I gave her a hug.

"Look babe you need to talk to your friend, I am freaking out here" I said immediately I got to the table

"I don't know what her problem is, ok so I went for our Annual meeting and just the first day of the meeting, I discovered she didn't bother to call me; her usual self would have called me to know how my trip went and all that, do you know I called her like three times and the response I got from those calls were horrific, at first I thought it was the pregnancy but........"

Sam interrupted me, "Temi I have tried not to talk about this because Kiki begged me not to, she wanted to handle it her own way, why are you cheating on her? Why Temi?"

"Sam what are you talking about?"

"What am I talking about?, ok which woman were you with that put an hotel address in your jacket, knowing it's your wife that will be doing the laundry"

My face rumpled with anger "Oh is it what this has been about, a note was found in my jacket and now I'm cheating on Kiki, couldn't you have asked me, if Kiki decided to be a child and think every man has to pay for her father's mistake, I am so disappointed in you I swear it Sam"

I got up and was leaving when Timi appeared and held my hands.

"Hey Temi, sit down please alright"

"Sweetie" he kissed his wife briefly and sat between them

"I'm sorry Temi" Samantha apologised,

"I am your sister and supposed to have talked to you about this"

"Yeah we are sorry" Timi added

"I was also aware but didn't just know how to come in until we figured out what to do yesterday night, I need you calm down, don't blame Kiki much alright, I think she's just been over sensitive considering her background, she loves you I think her fear is just getting the best of her, she hasn't fully let go of her past" Samantha said

"So bro how did the note get to our pocket, she saw a note that upset her so much"

"I don't know Sam, but I think I know who might have done this, remember the story I told you about high school, the girl I dated and how we met again in college of medicine in Alaska, she wanted us to continue the relationship but I had already given my life to Jesus and had made a promise to live my life for him, she tried all she could, even went as far as setting me up, I almost fell for her pranks but the Lord saved me, surprisingly sis! I met her again in AMDU New York and guess what she hasn't gotten over me.

"Does this mean anything to you"? I used my thump to touch the finger holding my wedding bound and waving it at her face"

She took a step backward and rolled her eyes.

"That doesn't mean anything to me Doctor Temi what has that gotten to do with our relationship Tee, look I don't mind sharing you with your wife".

"That will never happen" I screamed at her

Wow Sam stretched toward Temi, isn't she married yet?

I don't think so

"Omg" Timi said amidst laughter and hit the table "Marriage by force"

"You can say that again honey" Sam agreed holding her husband's arm

"Well at least I know what the problem is now, thanks Sam, Tim my guy thanks for this, I appreciate"

I said, got up and shook hands with Timi

"You welcome bro, I trust you know how to handle this, please make sure your decision doesn't hurt her alright?"

"Hurt her?" I said a half smile.

"That's like hurting me, I won't dare do something like that, I love her more than my own life"

"Very well then bro, we will be on our way now, your little friends will be waiting for us at school". Samantha said with a broad smile.

"O yeah that's true, you don't wanna see my little Spiderman's anger today do you?"

"No way" Samantha and Timi chorused.

We walked to the parking lot and exchanged hugs

"See you guys on Sunday"

"Alright bro, be good" I said and drove off.

Adenike Isenibi

CHAPTER
SIXTEEN

KIKI POV

"Stay here Kiki, I will be right back"

Aunty Bibi pointed to a long blue coach in a cute living room, small but well decorated and arranged.

Looking around, I saw a picture that looks so much like me when I was fifteen, what! I exclaimed this is me; I drew closer, wow Olami, Mum then the three of us together.

"Wait! Could this be mum's apartment?" I continued talking to myself. Wow mum in the states? am I dreaming?"

My lips parted as the door to my left side flow opened and I saw mom and Auntie Bibi coming out

"Huh!"

My eyes widened, she look so beautiful, her long hair is back, shining with little white touches all over, she was looking so much older than when we last saw but the pretty face glowing with grace like when were together long time ago

She stepped into my arms singing Kurt Carr's "I Almost let go

I almost let go

I felt like I couldn't just take life anymore

My problems had me bound

Depression weighed me down

But God held me close

So I wouldn't let go

God's mercy kept me

So I wouldn't let go

Auntie Jane and I joined her to sing the chorus

So I'm here today because God kept me

I'm alive today only because of his grace

Oh he kept me

So I wouldn't let go………

Tears flowing down our faces, we disengaged to seat, still holding her hands as if she was going to run and leave me again

We both sat staring at each other and said nothing, auntie Bibi left to give us time to talk

"What happened to us mom?" I broke the silence

"You were the a woman anyone would pray to have as a mother: loving, caring, beautiful, intelligent, spiritual, my role model and heroine but the death of Olami and dad's leaving us took all that away from me"

She smiled and held me to herself.

"I am very sorry honey, God is good. Your husband, Bibi and Mrs Onabanjo were God sent"

"My husband?" I asked in a very surprising tone

"Yes darling, your husband, hmmmm" she shook her head and continued talking

"That guy is the son I lost years ago, death took Olami and God gave him back to me as a son in law"

"Really?"

"Yeah" she stood up, walked to the window, looking outside she began her story.

"We were travelling to the village for our Christmas break many years ago when I was just eight, my father, my pregnant mother, I and my two other siblings. Suddenly my parents started screaming at each other as usual, *"boya emi ni Olorun to nshomo"* my mother shouted. *"Mi o bae pari wo fa, sha bi ti nue tan ko tu jobirin igba yen ni wa mo boya iwo loun shomo or not"* my father screamed back at her, I was going to ask them to stop shouting at each other few minutes later when our car seemed to be jumping, fear written on our parents face, my mother won't stop shouting and that was the last thing I could remember I found myself on the hospital bed and never saw my family again."

I was forced to live with my aged grandmother, who could do little or nothing to provide for us a decent meal, and she was always falling sick and feeble. My grandmother was a locust beans trader, locust beans takes a lot of hard work and long processing. At that time and age she could only do it once in a while because of the stress involved. I was very little; I couldn't do much to help maami. We struggled together and maami took care of me the little way she could. One day maami gave me palm kernel to go and hawk because she was very ill and we needed to pay some outstanding debt to mama Kemi (iya alagbo) and also get some agbo (herbs) to get her treated. My spirit refused to leave her to hawk that faithful day, I was moving sluggishly; I carried the tray of palm kernel and dropped it then go in to check on her again and again. Finally I made a small prayer for maami and left her to go so we will be able to pay for her agbo

I went quickly to the centre of the village to sell my palm kernel, before thirty minutes, I had finished selling and I rushed down to be with maam, but when I got home, I saw a small crowd in front of the house and everyone started giving me a strange look, I sensed danger, I ran inside before anyone could stop me. Maami was lying cold on the bed, she was dead. God, I thought I told you to keep maami for me, I cried. She was everything to me, my world crashed at her death. I became a village witch at a very tender age of ten; no one wanted to have anything to do with me"

"what!, but you were just a victim of circumstance" I said feeling some fresh tears gathering in my eyes

"Hmmmm" she smiled amidst tears

"Some said I killed my parents, siblings and now my grandmother, everyone in the village kept their distance, except Ojo my grandmother's mate's last child. Ojo was like three years older than me, he was the only friend I had, he would take me with him to his farm, gave me some of his farm products, I would eat, sell some of them to make some small amount to be able to buy books needed for my LEA primary school.

He started sleeping with me, he took my innocence, I

went through a lot of pains but couldn't complain because he was right about the only person I had. I finished my primary school at the age of eleven and wanted to take up maami's locust beans business when my uncle Martins who had been away for many years according to mama Ojo suddenly appeared in the village, one year after maami died.

Some of the villagers said he must be a ghost, some said he was mad, a lot was said about him but I had not seen nor heard about him before. The villagers filled maami's house to the brim....

Bo o le she rin Matini (martins why did you go like that) *iya yin jiya ko to ku o, haaa ese daa o*, they started accusing him, he wept and wept, everyone of them said different things and left one after the other.

Mama Ojo told him the whole story of how my parents died and how maami became bed ridden because of the death of my parents. He wept uncontrollably and promised mama Ojo to take me with him and will take good care of me.

Uncle Martins fulfilled his promise, he took me with him and took care of me, he was a very good man.

I started staying with his family, in Onitsha, a very nice place and a beautiful family; he had four boys and two girls. I became a sex slave to the boys, they will take turns in having sex with me on a daily basis, at first I would cry but then I became used to it. Not like I enjoyed it but I couldn't do anything to help myself. Hmmmm I blamed God for creating me to this world.

Uncle Martins saw me through secondary school and three of my baby uncles left for the university at the same time, thank you Lord I have only one to deal with now, I gave a sigh of relief

My uncle and auntie were very nice to me, they gave me money for my Jamb form, I sat for the exam and passed with flying colours. I was admitted into the higher institution at the same time with Oyewunmi their first daughter"

(She left the window and sat beside me, her eye balls looking weary.

She took a deep breath and continued)

"A dream come through was my first day at school, I was given a warm welcome at the girls hostel, where I would be sharing a room with three other girls. Then guys started rushing to me for relationships, somehow I always choose the wrong ones, getting in and out of relationships, immediately they got what they wanted they would leave me broken without looking back. None of them loved me or should I say none of them was ready to give me what I wanted, I was thirsty for love and looking for it in wrong places.

I sorrowfully bottled all the pains and heartbreaks, and then I tried to move on and never allow any man to hurt me ever again.

But unfortunately I made up mind too late"

She suddenly stopped talking; I drew closer and took her hands in mine

"Too late mum, how?"

"Hmmmm honey" she continued again,

"I made up my mind too late because I was already pregnant with your brother Olamiposi and was not even sure who the father was.

"What" My eyes widened

(She ignored the judgemental look written on my face and went on with her story)

"I was going to abort the pregnancy when I met your father at the hospital. We sat opposite each other at the hospital's reception where I was rehearsing what to tell the doctor, so will ll help me get rid of the obstacle growing in me. He kept staring at me, and then I stared back wondering why this good-looking, well dressed, young man could possibly be staring at a miserable lady like me.

As if he read my thought, he stood to seat by my side.

"Wow, I forgot what I came to the hospital to do"

"Hi pretty"

(I felt embarrassed) "Hello" I said in a whisper

"My name is Jake Johnson Olaobaju and I'm a banker working with the state bank"

"I am Derinsola Oyelami, I am a student at the state university studying secretarial studies"

He told me he came to see his mum, who was admitted into the hospital three days ago and asked me what I came to do. I lied to him that I also came to visit one of my course mates

Thereafter we could not stay off each other; we started sleeping together just three days after we met. I couldn't say No, I mean who would, to such a good-looking, kind hearted man like your father" *she paused and smiled*

"He swept me off my feet, from then on, everything went too fast and before I knew it, I was unable to tell him about my pregnancy and one month after he became the owner of the pregnancy "MD" (the pet name we gave to each other) I told him one night before we went to bed to tell him I was pregnant,

Ooooh I have never seen a man so happy like that, he carried me up and danced

"Thanks so much Dearie, so I'm going to be a father?" He took me to his mom, she was very happy to see me, when we told her I was pregnant she became more joyful, she received me as her own daughter, she didn't have a female child, she called me daughter and I called her maami.

We became very close and finally I found a family, a mother who loved me so much and a man who will do anything to make me happy.

I also took him to my uncle, where he paid the dowry, we rushed a small wedding and I became his wife.

I finally found the love I was looking for…..

Honey she squeezed my hands, your father made me a very happy woman. I went through the remaining of my programme with ease, I became the envy of many on campus, we were living large, I had my first car as a gift from your dad at the birth of your brother, I kept the secret to myself because I felt it was too late to tell your father and I didn't want to lose him"

"Baby" she bowed her head

"I hated myself, I hate meeting your dad at the time I did, I ruined our marriage before it started, I messed up his life because mine was in the toilet. It was such a terrible thing to do to a man like your dad, I was not fair to him at all"

I drew her to me and I gave her a hug.

"Calm down mom" I said quietly as the veins in my head were already on fire.

"Yeah baby", she disengaged and continued.

"Then four years later you came, the three of us received you with so much joy, I remembered Olami touching your curly full hair and said "God thank you for giving me a Cindarella as my little sister, she is so pretty" (*She said with a smile looking at our picture on the wall.*) "You grew to be very pretty and intelligent just like me, your daddy pampered us, he became the happiest man I have ever seen, he would wake up every morning to tell me how much he loved me and will never do anything to hurt me. Many years later, you were away at the boarding house, Olamiposi just got back from school after his 100 level's second semester exams. He fell ill and we took him to see Doctor Palmer. There we were told he needed blood and your father immediately offered to donate.

I did everything I could to stop him but he was too

stubborn and screamed at me that the life of his son is at stake.

He came back from the doctor's office looking so angry and refused to say a word to me.

I kept talking to him but he wouldn't even look at me

We were discharged the next morning

Immediately we got home, he helped Olami to his room and dragged me to our bed room

Gboaaa! gboaa!!, he gave me two hot slaps at once, I fell flat on the floor

He brought out bottle of wine from the fridge and started breaking them

Armed with half of the bottle in his hands, he was ready to stab me with it"

"Why didn't you tell me Derin why?" he screamed at me

"I knew what he was talking about immediately , I have never seen him like that before, he was very furious, his eyes were as red as blood, and he turned to a beast in just one second"

"I was going to tell you" I said on my knees.

"When? When? Answer me!! He barked at me, oooh is it

when he is about to get married and the real father of the groom shows up to claim his position huh?"

"I am sorry Jake, I am sorry"

"Don't call my name. You heartless woman"

"he ran after me with the broken bottle, Olami rushed into our room, towards us he slipped and fell on the broken bottle on the floor.

The bottle went straight into my boy's heart, your dad rushed towards him picked him up and we ran him to the hospital before they could do anything to help him, he looked into our eyes and said dad, mom I love you, tell Kiki that she will always remain my princess, I love her too and there in our hands he gave up."

"Your father screamed dropped him on the hospital floor and left me there. I was admitted in the hospital for three days in shock.

By the time I was discharged and got home, nothing that belonged to your father was remaining in the house, he left me too.

My whole life came to a standstill and I wondered why this always happens to me.

Why do all the people I love always end up leaving or dead?

So I decided to leave before you die or leave me too. I

couldn't take another heart attack. I prayed to God to take my life but he refused, I attempted suicide twice and something always happen and someone somewhere will come and rescue me.

I stopped praying, stopped going to church because I felt God hated me. I stopped talking to everyone about anything

I just buried myself in my work, making sure I avoid anything that will make me ask anyone for anything and also made sure no one had the courage to ask me for anything either"

She blew her nose with the handkerchief I gave her.

"Look darling, your husband is a good man, as I told you earlier he is the son I lost many years ago, he told us everything that happened, how you have been acting up and all. Look he told us nothing happened between him and the lady. That the lady was just trying to get his attention and he doesn't even have any idea that a note like that was inside his pocket. He refused to talk about it with you because you now started acting weird and he is also angry, baby

I want you to go get it right with your husband, tell him you are sorry and make sure he forgives you"

A flush of guilt rushed through my spine.

I should have talked to him about it, make him explain himself, now I have overreacted, I just hope I haven't destroyed my home, I hope I have not destroyed the beautiful gift God has given me, O God please forgive me, keep my home in the hollow of your hands I said a quick prayer in my thought.

"Honey" My mum continued

"Your husband brought me here and took me to a psychologist, Five months ago, I was just discharged one month ago, he drove me straight to this place, right now, as am talking to you I have my own shop where I sew with 4 people working for me and none of these four collects less than 300 dollars at the end of the week, what more can one ask from a son in law"

I started sweating in my grey Tuttle neck sweater

OMG Temi, now I see why he has been guarding his phone jealously

"Look at me dearie, am I not looking good" *she showed off her well tailored caftan,*

"I made this myself" she said proudly

"and I am going to be making for you, my son Temi, my handsome grandson and my little one inside, she robbed my swollen tummy"

"Talking about your grandson mum, do you know Alex actually told us he met you in Auntie Bibi's house?"

"my mummy Bibi's nice friend said I'm gonna to be a cool pilot and guess what mum she somehow looks like you" I mimicked Alex

"Mum we didn't take him seriously because we thought he was just excited spending the weekend with Auntie Bibi who is always spoiling him"

"Yeah Bibi brought the little boy to me that day at the rehab, I was already coming out of my misery, she introduced him to me and I hugged the boy so tight and hid my tears, I was so excited we went to Bibi's for the weekend and I returned on Sunday evening"

"I was in church when you led this Sunny Badu's song ermm"

"If this is your power" I helped her out

"Yeah honey that's the song, Bibi couldn't stay because she needed to take me back that day to the rehab"

"Jesus Christ mom that is very correct, I should have known because she never misses our Sunday afternoon coffee"

"Awwwwwww you people"

"Samantha's mom did a great job honey"

"I can't be more grateful to God, your sweet husband, Mrs. Onabanjo and of course a friend like Bibi"

I hugged her again and again,

"I can't still believe you are here with us, I am so happy mom" I wept again

"Don't tell me that Samantha is part of this too mom?"

"No way, honey that girl can't keep her mouth shut to save her soul when it concerns you; she would have told you everything if she knew" she said and laughed.

"Her mom practically warned every one of them not to let her in"

"You see dear" she became serious again

"Marriage is a very hard work, it is like walking a long distant, if you made the commitment then be ready to take up the cross, it is not a bed of roses"

"It is an everlasting institution where new things keeps coming up, you have so many things to deal with in marriage, your husband, your children, your in laws and career. It is not just like I love him/her, love is never enough; it is a lot of work for the two of you if you really want it to workout

First you must be as transparent as a see through glass, pretend that your husband is God who can see everything, so you won't be tempted to keep anything away from him and let him know that you do trust him"

"But mum, I'm trying, it's not as if I have hidden anything from him….."

"I know baby, you have not, I mean I have myself to blame for abandoning you and chasing your father away from us.

There's no how you won't be over sensitive, you might not want to have a full trust in men, for the fear of the unknown, but baby I am sure you know now that your father is not the problem, I am" fresh tears falling down her face.

"It's alright mom stop please" I said as I wiped her tears with my thumb.

"Please baby you have to trust your husband, trust is the foundation in which marriage is built, when the trust isn't there then the foundation is faulty and if the foundation is faulty then marriage is about to crash, your marriage will not crash Kiki"

"Amen"

"Another very important thing is friendship, it's really very important; someone you can get silly with, that you can talk about everything and anything with, don't take life too seriously my love, I have seen the other side of life and I can tell you it's not a sweet experience"

"I will be right back honey" she dashed quickly to her room and returned with a small book that look like a jotter

"Now sweetheart I want you to go and make your marriage work" she gave me a pat at the back and handed me the small book

"Ok mom, what is this about?"

"It is a letter from me to you"

"Alrite mom",

"Jeez! I am thirty minutes late, your grandson is still in school"

"Haaaa ok dear *oya teetee malo, ma gbagbe ko ka iwe yen o*"

"*Beni ma*" I gave her another hug and ran out to the escalator

"We are all coming tomorrow mum" I said as the escalator door closed

I rushed to pick Alex from school, Jeez 45minutes late

I sped down the lane, lost in my thought, how will I face you now Temi"

"Sorry son, I am late"

He eyed me hugging himself

"You have been coming late since on Monday mum" he said refusing to hug me.

"Awwww Alex you too" I thought

"Ok sorry my love pleaseeeeeeeeee" I said pretending to be crying

He rushed to me and hugged me

"Ok mum don't cry I'm not mad at you anymore"

"Are you sure?" I asked still covering my face with my hands

"Yes mum" he screamed

"Okay, what do you want mummy to get for you? We will be on our way to the mall now"

"yeeepie" he jumped into the back seat and started giving me a long list of items he has been dying to get.

"Okay son done"

After our long list of items for bribe were purchased my excited son shouted

"Thank you mom, I love you"

"I love you more my king"

"No mom I love you more"

"Ok son you love me more" we hugged and headed back home.

Adenike Isenibi

CHAPTER
SEVENTEEN

I *have always tried to be a model for you of what it is to be a good wife. After all these years I am still in love with your father, more than ever. I pray you will be very happy in your marriage.*

I would like to give you an advice and hope you will take it to heart, it comes from deep inside my soul, I have not always done the right things. Your dad and I have had our troubles along the way that we had to go our separate ways, most of what was the mistakes I made but I have learned a lot. I have asked God for forgiveness, he has forgiven me I am sure of that but I still have the scare, you will not learn from your own bad experience in Jesus name.

Say "I love you" often and show it even more often. Hug,

kiss and hold hands. God made this man for you to love and to hold, never turn your husband down for love making. He won't go anywhere else if he is fed well at home. Be playful, make it fun and make it interesting.

Say "thank you" for the things that he does for you, anywhere he takes you, show gratitude by saying thank you and acknowledge his effort.

Be kind and sweet. Never cut him down in front of people especially your children. This will hurt him deeper than anything. Let him have his male pride even when you think he's wrong. Hold your tongue it is better to be wrong than to be right.

Think the best of him. Speak the best about him to others. Keep a mental rolodex of his shining moments. Draw on those memories when life gets hard. It will help pull you through the rough patches every marriage has.

Allow him to do his job – lead, provide and protect you in the best way he knows how. Don't stand in his way or rise up against him. I know he will do his job as I have seen him taken charge and doing these things in your life already. Your calling is to be honest with him and respective towards him.

Right now it seems easy to do these things but there will come times when it will be hard. Be honest even when he will not like to hear the truth. Say anything you want to say in a respective manner. This will get you a long way. Children learn disobedience, dishonesty and disregard from their mother's example towards their father. Remember you choose him and God made him your leader through the covenant of marriage.

Love him more than you love your children. Don't put your children in front him in your life. Women were created because men needed them, not primarily for children. Children are an example of you and your husband's living breathing love.

Still keep having private time alone together. Laugh together, share secrets and have fun as a couple.

Stand by him when he disciplines your children. Never pick up and cuddle them after punishment until they have made up with their father. Up hold his rules and leadership of the family. Remember he has veto power in all decisions. Never disagree with him in front of the children. Present a united front. You can voice your concerns at a more private time.

My grandma always said, "women go to men for strength. "lean on him. Need him. Listen to him; men go to women for comfort. A clean house, good meal, soft kind words, back rubs, sex always comfort him. Never make him sorry he came home to you.

You can come and tell me anything you want. I'm

your mother and love you very much. But as long as your husband is doing his job (leading, providing and protecting you) I will never build a case against him to you. I will always direct you back to him. He is to be the head and you're his heart.

I think you have a good man. Treat him like one and he will always act like one. He will lay the moon and stars at your feet for your pleasure. And you will be in his heart forever.

I love you very much and I am proud of the woman you have grown up to be. I can't wait to see how God writes the rest of your life story. I will be praying for you every day

Love

Mom

"Wow! Thank you mom" I said gratefully to myself after reading the letter she gave me with undivided attention

I rushed out to make dinner myself I asked Jude to make sure Alex had his dinner and prepare him for bed.

I decorated the dining table with dinner candles, his favourite wine chilling in a bowl of iced block, and of course, The "I am sorry card" I got from the mall.

I wanted to have time alone with Temi, I was waiting patiently for him to return, he took longer than expected

I was beginning to get worried when the door bell announced his arrival, I rushed to open the door, gave him a hug and he reluctantly hugged me back

He drew back some minutes later when he noticed I wasn't letting go and said "what is happening here?"

I ignored the surprise written over his cute face

"I made us dinner" I said, leaving me standing he headed straight upstairs to the bedroom

"I am not hungry" he said not looking at me at all

I stood in front of the door brimming with thoughts of what to tell him, oh Lord how do I start, what do I tell him.

"I desperately need to talk to you Temi" I said finally as I got the courage to enter the room.

He turned to me with a stern look, shook his head and dashed into the bathroom.

I sat on the bed waiting for him, he got into his pyjamas and laid on the bed playing with his I pad.

"Babieeeee please naw"

It was obvious he didn't want to talk to me, I didn't blame him, I have disappointed him by behaving the way I did, he would have asked me and would have accepted my explanation for it, if it were him.

"Well it's not totally my fault, I was scared that what happened to my mum was going to repeat itself in my marriage, I was only preparing for the worse in case. I mean I don't want to be miserable, if it eventually happens, I don't want to wake up one morning and find out I am no longer beautiful and I have lost my brain because of a man, I don't wanna kill myself before I die just because a man has decided to leave me, no I don't want to"

"Come on baby please" I joined him on the bed

"Forgive me"

"Kiki I don't think I wanna talk to you right now, please can we do this tomorrow I had a long day alright"

"Tomorrow Temi?"

"Don't tell me you are so mad at me that you will waste my food, look I made it myself with this big tommy, ok just come and eat and we talk about this tomorrow alright"

He agreed reluctantly and I led us downstairs

I handed him the card and held him to push further with my appeal.

He read and looked at me

"What was this weeks of madness about Kiki, I thought we were friends; I thought we could talk about anything.

A note that I didn't even know was there would have broken us up Kiki, couldn't we have talked about it and you know very well that I won't do such to you. I won't deceive you; I am really disappointed in you"

I felt embarrassed and tears started rushing out of my eyes as he stood up to hold me.

"It ok babes don't cry I forgive you, don't let this happen again please, do you understand?"

"Yes my love"

"I love you so much Kiki "

"I love you too Temi"

We held each other and I knew that this is my place; this is where I belong in your arms, in your world Doctor Greg.

THE END